SOCIAL PARANOIA:

HOW CONSUMERS AND BRANDS CAN STAY SAFE IN A CONNECTED WORLD

DANE COBAIN

Edited by Pam Elise Harris
Cover Design by Stephanie Stacker

INTRODUCTION

SOCIAL NETWORKING SITES can be scary places. When the whole world is connected, anything can happen, and it can happen quickly, too. Just consider the case of Justine Sacco, the PR executive who was fired after posting a racist tweet when boarding a plane[1]. Sacco went offline for eleven hours during the flight, only to find out that her post had gone viral and she'd been fired whilst in the air.

The speed of social networking has its upsides. After all, a world of information is at your fingertips. I'll always remember the first time I saw the power of Twitter, when people were posting updates from the London riots in 2009, literally hours before the same information was being broadcast by the news channels.

But it has its downsides, too. These days, anyone can accidentally become a meme or unwittingly star in a viral video. Remember the Star Wars Kid[2]? His name is Ghyslain Raza, and he went viral at the age of fifteen after starring in a video where he twirled a golf ball retriever around like a lightsaber. Raza never intended for the video to go public, but he accidentally left the tape lying around and it was discovered by three of his schoolmates, who digitised it and distributed it online.

Raza has said that he was a victim of cyberbullying because the video attracted a number of negative comments. His family filed a lawsuit against the families of the kids who uploaded it, and Raza has since started using the video to speak out against bullies and cyberbullying.

And it's not just individuals who can fall victim to a social networking scandal. It can happen to brands as well, and it's arguably more noticeable

---

[1] See: http://www.theguardian.com/world/2013/dec/22/pr-exec-fired-racist-tweet-aids-africa-apology

[2] See: http://knowyourmeme.com/memes/star-wars-kid

when it does happen. Just think about the backlash against Celeb Boutique when they hijacked the #Aurora hashtag with the message, "#Aurora is trending, clearly about our Kim K inspired #Aurora dress ;)"

No, Celeb Boutique. #Aurora was trending because James Eagan Holmes walked into a midnight screening of *The Dark Knight Rises* in Aurora, Colorado, and then killed twelve people. No one was in the mood to buy a dress.

Then there's the infamous case of Dell Hell with blogger Jeff Jarvis, and the time when Dave Carroll went viral for writing a song called "United Breaks Guitars" about his troubles with the airline. Sure, people have every right to be paranoid about using social networking sites, but so do brands. It's a minefield out there, especially if you're unprepared.

I could go on and on, but that's what the rest of the book is for. I'll talk to you about the different ways that social networking can make you vulnerable, and I'll tell you how to protect yourself. After all, used responsibly, social networking sites are a great way to keep up with your family and friends, as well as with the rest of the world.

Along the way, you'll learn from a number of case studies, each of which is categorised depending upon which aspect of social media is to blame – from hacks and leaks to viral videos and the legacy that you leave behind.

Social Paranoia: How to Stay Safe in a Connected World is the result of years of industry experience and a survey which was conducted in 2015 to gauge the thoughts and opinions of real people. You can read more about that in the appendix. In the meantime, make sure no one's looking over your shoulder and read on.

Oh, and don't forget to post about the book on your social networking site of choice… if you dare.

CONTENTS

CHAPTER ONE: WHAT IS SOCIAL PARANOIA?

THIS SEEMS LIKE the logical place to start, right? Social paranoia is the feeling you get when you hesitate before posting an update. It's the feeling you get on a Saturday morning after drunkenly texting your ex the night before. The feeling you get when your friends won't stop posting about their perfect lives, making your own life seem dull in comparison.

If that sounds like you, you're not alone. Social paranoia is a real phenomenon, and it affects more people than you might expect. After all, social networking sites are relatively new, although you could argue that, as a species, we've been forming social networks since the dawn of time.

And so, to some extent, social paranoia is already manifest in the form of social anxiety disorder. Social anxiety disorder is one of the most common forms of anxiety disorder, and it typically involves an excessive and unreasonable fear of social situations. It's easy to see how social networking, which is, after all, an extension of interpersonal relationships, could bring on a similar sense of unease.

But social paranoia is more than that. It's something that affects us all, although it affects some of us more than others. A couple of years ago, I wrote an article for Adweek[3] about a hoax that was making the rounds. A horde of angry mothers descended upon a page about "babies," leaving angry messages for the pervert who'd stolen their kids' photos and put them up on a Facebook page.

Except that's not quite what happened. The page was automatically generated, and it only showed photos if you already had access to look at them. If the parents hadn't uploaded the photos, no one would have been

---

[3] See: http://www.adweek.com/socialtimes/people-arent-stealing-your-facebook-photos-a-lesson-in-privacy/421081

able to see them. They were at fault, not some shady guy in an ice-cream van.

Case Study: A *Fake Review on Amazon*
Classification: *Other People*

What Happened:

A month after the release of my debut novella, *No Rest for the Wicked*, I was taking a look at the Amazon reviews when I noticed a brand new, one-star review. As a writer, I'm always keen to learn from constructive criticism, so I decided to take a look at it.

It turned out that the "review" was actually a thinly disguised personal attack, published under a fake name and spouting false allegations in an attempt to discredit me.

It wasn't difficult to track down the culprit – someone I'd never even met, but who held a vendetta against me. Without some detective work, I would never have guessed it was him because he was so far removed from me, but that doesn't make much difference in the age of the internet.

How it Could've Been Avoided:

In this instance, there was no way to avoid it. It was an unprovoked attack from someone I wasn't connected to in the first place. Fortunately, the fake review was reported to Amazon and subsequently removed with no permanent damage.

Authors are paranoid enough about negative reviews. After all, a book is like a child, and it's always tough when someone criticises it. Add the possibility of fake negative reviews to sit alongside the genuine ones, and it's a surprise that more writers aren't sitting in padded cells and ranting about social networking sites and the people who use them.

Back at the tail end of 2014, Crowdedbrain published an article referring to the year as "the year of social media paranoia,"[4] revealing new research that claimed that three-quarters of Brits suffer from social paranoia, and that young people (aged eighteen to twenty-one) are the most paranoid of all. Worse, when asked how that compared to the previous year, 61% of respondents said that their social paranoia was worse than ever before.

Interestingly, the same survey found that women are more paranoid then men, and that a quarter of people (24%) are paranoid that they might get caught looking through old photos and status updates. Sixteen percent of people are paranoid because of their inability to trust their partner to behave themselves on social media.

Note the contrast here. A fear of being caught looking through old updates is unique to social networking, but spousal mistrust is as old as time itself.

Google, the dictionary of choice for millennials, defines paranoia as an "unjustified suspicion and mistrust of other people"[5]. Whilst it's easy to be unjustly suspicious in the age of social networking, it's also true that sometimes people are out to get you.

Despite this, we shouldn't be scared of social networking. After all, used responsibly, social networking sites can help you to stay up-to-date with your family and friends, and the positives (usually) outweigh the negatives.

Paranoia could be more common than you thought. According to British psychologist Daniel Freeman, one in four Londoners suffers from paranoid thoughts on a regular basis[6]. As if that weren't enough, paranoid thoughts are on the rise in both the UK and the US.

Freeman believes that city life itself can lead to paranoia. Because we constantly make split-second decisions based on limited information such as which street to take or whether a stranger is dangerous, our decision-making processes are prone to error.

If this is true, it's easy to see how the same thing could be happening

---

[4] See: http://www.crowdedbrain.co.uk/news/mobile-news/three-quarters-of-britons-suffer-from-social-media-paranoia.html

[5] See: https://www.google.co.uk/search?q=define%3Aparanoia

[6] See: http://www.livescience.com/3064-freak-paranoia-common.html

online. After all, the internet is virtually infinite, and there's never enough time to see everything. In fact, researchers in Canada found that internet users make decisions in "the blink of an eye."[7]

"My colleagues believed it would be impossible to really see anything in less than 500 milliseconds," explained Gitte Lindgaard of Ottawa's Carleton University, one of the researchers involved in the project. Instead, they found that first impressions were established in just fifty milliseconds, which is roughly the length of a single frame of television footage.

If being forced to make a number of split-second decisions can lead to paranoia, it stands to reason that fast-paced social networking sites such as Twitter, where you're inundated with information and have to choose what to focus on, could have the same effect.

One recent survey found that almost two-thirds of social networkers have lied to "airbrush reality,"[8] to make their lives seem more interesting than they actually are. In fact, psychologists have warned that people might suffer from digital amnesia by starting to believe their own version of events and forgetting what actually happened.

The same survey also found that nearly half of people feel paranoia, sadness and shame as a result of not being able to live up to the image that they've created. Dr. Richard Sherry, a clinical psychologist and a founding member of the Society for Neuropsychoanalysis, believes that these feelings of guilt and distaste towards ourselves can lead to psychological problems such as anxiety.

"Our need to document and share our lives is part of our nature," he explains. "But the strengths and drawbacks of social media need to be understood better by society. Being competitive is normal. However, the dark side of this social conformity is when we negate what authentically feels to be 'us' to the degree that we no longer recognise the memory or the view of ourselves."

But if that's the case, would we be better off if we abstained from social media altogether? Well, that depends. What kind of person are you? I asked

---

[7] See: http://www.nature.com/news/2006/060109/full/news060109-13.html

[8] See: http://www.dailymail.co.uk/health/article-2888454/Youngsters-airbrushing-reality-social-media-make-lives-interesting-suffer-paranoia-sadness-shame-fail-live-online-image.html

our survey respondents whether they considered themselves to be introverts or extroverts; 51.5% were introverts, 20.7% were extroverts, and the remaining 27.8% sat somewhere in between.

Introverts and extroverts use social networking sites in different ways. I'm an extrovert, and I largely use social networking sites to get the word out about my writing and to promote myself as a writer, a musician and a poet. Introverts, however, are more likely to be cautious, and they typically try to avoid drawing attention to themselves.

Introverts are much more likely to lurk on social networking sites, reading other people's updates without posting anything themselves. These are the people who typically experience feelings of paranoia because of their belief that their own lives are less interesting than the lives of their friends.

But extroverts are the folks who keep exaggerating the facts. An introvert wouldn't bother lying because they don't want attention in the first place. This suggests that extroverts could be more vulnerable to false memories and the problems with anxiety that Dr. Sherry talked about earlier in this chapter.

TOP DEFINITION

fomo

"fear of missing out". The fear that if you miss a party or event you will miss out on something great

Even though he was exhausted, John's fomo got the best of him and he went to the party.

by Beaqon October 02, 2006

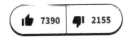 

(Source: UrbanDictionary.com)

And there's another potential problem – fear of missing out, a phenomenon which is as old as human society. Fear of missing out, or FOMO, affects us all to some extent, and you see it in all areas of life, not just on social media.

For example, some people play the National Lottery every week, even though they've never won anything because they're worried that if they stop playing their numbers will come up. That's a classic case of FOMO, and a great example of how it works in the real world.

When it comes to social networking, FOMO can affect you in different ways. Some people spend all of their time logged into Facebook, endlessly scrolling their newsfeeds in case they've missed something. Others are obsessed with checking the latest trending topics on Twitter, and some people are so desperate to stay up-to-date that they cyberstalk specific friends on a regular basis so that they don't miss a single post.

Of course, the rapid speed of social networking means that you can never stay up-to-date with it. You can't watch every video on YouTube, for example, because one hundred hours of new video is uploaded every minute.

The key is to accept this fact and to move on. Besides, if your FOMO gets so bad that you're forced to sit in front of a smartphone all day, you'll miss out on reality. As with most things, the key is moderation. Otherwise, you're at risk of becoming a paranoid consumer.

CHAPTER TWO: PARANOID CONSUMERS

A CONSUMER IS a person who purchases goods and services, which means that we're all consumers whether we like it or not. In our modern age, it's impossible to live our lives without consuming products and services on a daily basis.

A brand, meanwhile, is a name, a term, a design or a symbol that sets one product apart from another. Branding originated on cattle ranches, when ranchers would brand a symbol onto each of their animals to prove ownership. We'll take a closer look at brands in later chapters.

Consumer paranoia is often a result of some action that the person has taken. For example, someone might post a contentious political status and then start to worry about who might have seen it and how they might have reacted.

Case Study: *Britain First Takes Advantage of Kids*
Classification: *Virality*

What Happened:

Two men acting on behalf of far-right organisation Britain First took a photo of themselves guarding two poppy-selling sea cadets against "Islamic extremists." However, the two girls, who were aged twelve and thirteen, didn't know who the men were, and they had to fight to get the photo removed from Facebook after Britain First posted it as part of a propaganda piece.

Nottingham Sea Cadets was also forced to reassure the public that they don't support Britain First and that their employees were working hard to have the photo removed. Britain First, meanwhile, refused to comment.

How it Could've Been Avoided:

Unfortunately, the girls found themselves in a tricky situation. Once a photo like that has been posted, it's difficult to get it removed. Even if it was removed, there was nothing to stop Britain First's henchmen from reposting it. However, the girls' parents and the Nottingham Sea Cadets responded wisely by lobbying Facebook to remove the images and by distancing themselves from both the incident and the group.

One study found that whilst personal Twitter posts made people appear to be more trustworthy, these trustworthy users paradoxically received lower levels of interaction[9]. Therefore, if you make a habit of posting personal updates, it's easy to see how you might get less interaction from your friends and family and why you might start to feel paranoid as a result.

The most important thing that you can do to protect yourself is to adopt the Grandma Rule. Simply put, before you post something on a social networking site, ask yourself whether you'd be comfortable if your grandma saw it.

Alternatively, ask yourself what your boss might say, or a potential employer in the future. If in doubt, don't post it. Remember, nothing's ever truly private on the internet.

---

[9] See: http://www.forbes.com/sites/michaelthomsen/2015/10/16/new-study-suggests-personal-twitter-posts-decrease-social-interaction/

Case Study: *Carly McKinney Gets Fired*
Classification: *Legacy*

What Happened:

Former maths teacher Carly McKinney was fired from her job at Overland High School in Aurora, Colorado, after a series of inappropriate tweets caught the attention of local station 9News and led to her suspension.

The twenty-three-year-old posted a number of semi-naked photographs of herself, as well as multiple drug references. One photo was captioned, "Naked. Wet. Stoned."

One article by CBS[10] pointed out that even though a teacher has a First Amendment right to freedom of speech on social networking sites, the district's recommendation is to treat social media in the same way that you'd treat a classroom. A statement from a district spokeswoman added that "the three posts [they were] most concerned about [were] the ones that may indicate that she violated school policy and/or law."

How it Could've Been Avoided:

This situation could have been avoided completely if Carly had used the Grandma Rule. It's important to remember that the widespread proliferation of social networking sites means that your private and public identities are no longer separate. And that's bad news if you thought that adding "views are my own" to your bio means that you can say whatever you like. It's effectively meaningless and offers you no protection

---

[10] See: http://denver.cbslocal.com/2013/03/22/teacher-center-racy-tweets-school-district/

whatsoever.

Using the Grandma Rule doesn't mean that you can't be yourself. It just means you should be a little more careful. After all, when you hang out with your grandparents, you're still the same person that you are when you hang out with your friends. You just tone it down and avoid mentioning things that they're better off not knowing.

Social networking is the same. If you embrace the contentious by sharing religious or political subject matter, you're likely to provoke a response.

On an anecdotal level, I often find that we hang around with people with similar beliefs, whether we're talking about religious beliefs or political ideologies. When it comes to social networking, your circle of friends tends to be much larger, and your potential reach is larger, too. Because of this, it's a lot easier to cause offence.

Luckily, most social networking sites allow you to customise your privacy settings, helping you to ensure that your updates are only seen by certain people. Privacy settings aren't foolproof, but they do help you to keep your information safe. Unfortunately, mistakes can still be made.

Case Study: *BuzzFeed's Editor-in-Chief Makes a Mistake*
Classification: *Privacy*

What Happened:

In August 2015, Ben Smith, BuzzFeed's Editor-in-Chief, accidentally tweeted a screenshot of a private conversation that had been taking place in his direct messages[11]. Smith had been talking to a reporter from The Intercept, who was planning on leaving the publication. In the leaked conversation, he was pictured enquiring about vacancies at BuzzFeed.

Smith told The Next Web, who covered the story, that he was "mortified"

---

[11] See: http://thenextweb.com/media/2015/08/07/bad-buzz/

about the incident and that he discovered the offending screenshot on his mobile phone after searching for it.

It's remarkably difficult to take a screenshot and to tweet it without meaning to, but as we have no reason to doubt Smith's word, we have to assume that he's telling us the truth.

Smith quickly deleted the tweet, and most publications were respectful enough to omit the name of the journalist. But in the age of the internet, it's impossible to truly delete something. Let's just hope that the guy didn't lose his job. At least, not before he managed to find a new one.

How it Could've Been Avoided:

This is a tricky one because there's not much that the journalist could have done. If anything, Smith should figure out how the accident happened so that he can stop it from happening again.

That said, the journalist could have saved himself a lot of trouble if he'd spoken to Smith on the phone or via e-mail. This is a perfect example of the convenience of social networking leading to less of a focus on security. One thing's for sure. They'll both be more careful with their messages in the future.

This case study is a perfect illustration of the importance of having a plan in place so that you know what to do if something goes wrong. As a high-profile public figure, it's likely that Smith was all too aware of the scrutiny that his tweets would be under, and so he was able to react quickly once he realised his mistake.

It's hard to give specific advice on what to do when something bad happens because it depends upon the circumstances. If you've been hacked, for example, then you'll want to change your passwords and to run scans for viruses. If a photo of you goes viral then you're more likely to want to tighten up your privacy settings.

However, there are a number of things to keep up your sleeves, just in case. Consider updating your privacy settings so that your profiles and updates are visible only to your friends. This is particularly useful if you're on the receiving end of unwanted attention. The last thing that you want is for people to dig up even more dirt when you're already under scrutiny.

On top of this, if people pounce upon a mistake that you make, apologise. Even if your words were taken out of context, just apologise. You'd be surprised at how much of a difference an apology can make.

Case Study: *Family Wrongly Targeted in Noah Thomas Backlash*

Classification: Privacy

What Happened:

After the death of 5-year-old Noah Thomas, an offensive post about the tragedy went viral on Facebook. As a result, some self-appointed vigilantes posted what was ostensibly the address that the offensive post originated from.

Unfortunately, the address actually belonged to Roni Boswell, who lived there with her husband and her three-year-old son. The Boswells had nothing to do with the post, but that didn't stop three thousand people from sharing their address. The Boswells even had to get the local police involved after people started arriving at their front door to demand answers.

How it Could've Been Avoided:

Unfortunately, cases like this can be hard to police. After all, how do you stop someone else from sharing your address? Even if your address isn't listed online, you could still be unlucky enough to have it picked out at random.

In the Boswells' case, they did the best that they could, by informing the local police force and putting a sign on the door to explain what had happened. However, the negative attention was so great that they were forced to leave their house and to stay elsewhere until the furore died down.

Depending upon the severity of the situation, you might want to encourage your friends and family to update their settings, too. After all, internet commenters are notoriously aggressive and, in some cases, people have been on the receiving end of abuse despite doing nothing at all to deserve it.

If you were to write a list of every social networking trend and to rank them in order of their likelihood of causing paranoia, the trend of sexting (i.e. sending explicit photographs of yourself via SMS or instant messaging) would have to be at the top.

It's pretty obvious why sexting is a bad idea. After all, once you've sent something to someone, it's out of your hands. Of course you're going to feel paranoid if you know that all of your exes have photos of your genitals. Want to avoid being paranoid? Don't send photos of your genitals to people!

Over the last couple of years, there's been an explosion in the growth of "revenge porn" sites, which allow people to share pornographic photographs and videos of their former partners. It's illegal, but that doesn't stop people from doing it.

As we've discussed elsewhere, once someone else has access to your files, you're no longer in control. It's incredibly difficult to get something removed from a revenge porn website. Even the police are unable to do much to help. In most cases, authorities focus on arresting the owners and operators of these websites, rather than the people who upload the images.

That said, in November 2015, damages were awarded in a sexting case for the first time in British history[12] The case was brought about after a girl was encouraged to send sexually-explicit photographs of herself to a teacher. The judge eventually awarded £25,000 to the victim for the psychological harm that was caused.

---

[12] See: http://www.bbc.co.uk/news/uk-34716852

Case Study: *Kevin Bollaert Goes to Jail*
Classification: Other People

What Happened:

Kevin Bollaert of San Diego, California, created a website called UGotPosted.com, which allowed people to post sexual photography of their former partners. By definition, each of these photographs was uploaded without the victim's consent, and Bollaert charged people up to $350 to get the photos removed.

Bollaert was convicted in February of 2015 on twenty-one counts of ID theft and six of extortion. He was later sentenced to eighteen years in jail and ordered to pay $15,000 to the victims, as well as a $10,000 fine.

How it Could've Been Avoided:

Bollaert could have avoided the situation by not breaking the law in the first place. The victims, however, could only have avoided the situation by not taking the compromising photos.

In the end, social networking has created a culture in which nothing is private. It's no wonder that paranoia is becoming increasingly common. After all, people keep secrets for a reason, and social networking is making it harder and harder for people to hide things from their friends and family.

Even the basic functionality of some websites can cause a problem. For example, WhatsApp shows you the last time that a user was active, as well as whether they've received your messages or not. That's usually not a problem, but there are exceptions. For example, if you tell someone that your phone is out of battery but they see that you were recently active, they're going to know that you were lying.

In many ways, social networking is the great leveller. A machine or an algorithm won't deliberately reveal your secrets because you can't be deliberate unless you're sentient. However, they might catch you out when you're already doing something that you're not supposed to be doing.

Which brings me on to my main piece of advice for anyone who's trying to avoid feelings of social paranoia. Just don't do anything you're not supposed to do. That should protect you in most instances, but not all of them – not when it comes to hacks and leaks, for example.

CHAPTER THREE: HACKS AND LEAKS

THERE ARE A LOT of misconceptions about hacking. Despite the negative connotations, not all hackers are out to get you. In fact, a lot of companies, such as Google and Facebook, host official internal hackathons.

Hackathons typically last for twenty-four to forty-eight hours, and they involve filling a room with computer programmers and unleashing their creativity. The goal is usually to create a working prototype of a piece of software by "hacking" different bits of code. Many websites offer application programming interfaces (APIs), which competing developers are able to use to create new services from existing data.

But in popular culture, we tend to think of hackers as long-haired computer nerds who are able to bypass security systems and to access data without authorisation. It's true that this type of hacker exists. It's just that they don't do it like they do it in the movies.

Leaks are a little different, although hacks and leaks go hand-in-hand. A hacker might gain access to a social networking profile and post some bogus updates, for example, or they might read through your conversations. If that's all that they do, it's a hack.

A leak occurs when a hacker gains access to a database and then releases its contents. Because of this, leaks are usually much more high profile. A hack might involve just one account, whilst a leak has the potential to affect millions. Let's look at a case study.

Case Study: *Ashley Madison Leak*
Classification: *Hacks and Leaks*

What Happened:

Ashley Madison is a dating site that's owned by Avid Life Media and which aims to facilitate extramarital affairs, using the tagline, "Life is short. Have an affair." As you can imagine, most of its users aren't keen on broadcasting their membership. So when hackers gained access to the website's database, all hell broke loose.

It's interesting to note that the hack was reported several weeks before the files were released. When the data was finally released, by a collective of hackers called the Impact Group, it was accompanied by a statement:

"Time's up! Avid Life Media has failed to take down Ashley Madison and Established Men. We have explained the fraud, deceit, and stupidity of ALM and their members. Now everyone gets to see their data."

It's estimated that up to thirty-seven million people were affected, and analysis of the data has been able to tie e-mail addresses back to multiple high-profile figures. Self-identified hacker @T0x0 found more than 6,700 US Army e-mail addresses, 1,600 from the Navy, 104 from the Virginia state government and 45 from the Department of Homeland Security.

Ultimately, the scandal had a human cost. Police in Canada eventually released details of two suicides that were related to the incident.[13].

---

[13] See: http://www.bbc.co.uk/news/technology-34044506

How it Could've Been Avoided:

Unfortunately, there's not a huge amount that users could have done, although they could have used fake names and e-mail addresses on the service. However, credit card fragments were also leaked, which would be harder for people to fake. You could also argue that it's their own fault for joining an infidelity site in the first place.

Whilst the hackers themselves are the primary culprit, Avid Life Media is responsible for safeguarding its members' data. It's not always possible to prevent a hack, but steps can be taken to ensure that all data is encrypted and stored securely.

Fortunately, leaks are relatively uncommon. Just 10.4% of our survey respondents have been affected by one. Admittedly, this was before the Ashley Madison hack, but that's not the only website to have ever leaked information.

In fact, at the time of writing, HaveIBeenPwned.com reports that 53 major websites and over 220 million accounts have been affected, including 150 million Adobe accounts, 4.5 million Snapchat accounts and 1.3 million YouPorn accounts.

Let's take a closer look at the Snapchat leak.

Case Study: *Fappenings and Snappenings*
Classification: *Hacks and Leaks*

What Happened:

On August 31st 2014, approximately five hundred private photographs of celebrities were uploaded to 4chan. They were later disseminated elsewhere, including on Imgur, Reddit and Tumblr. The hackers are believed to have accessed the images by exploiting a weakness in Apple's iCloud in a targeted attack on specific accounts.

The leak was dubbed" The Fappening," and a number of high-profile figures were affected including Jennifer Lawrence, Kate Upton and Kirsten Dunst. The initial leak was followed up by two further leaks, which included further photographs and videos of celebrities.

Then, in October of the same year, tens of thousands of images and videos shared by Snapchat users were released online after being stored by a third-party website. Disturbingly, many of the images could be classified as child pornography, thanks to the app's predominantly underage user-base and the fact that it has a reputation as a platform for sexting.

How it Could've Been Avoided:

This one's pretty simple. Never, ever make a sex tape, and if you do make a sex tape, make sure it's never digitised. As soon as something is digitised, it's vulnerable, especially if it's digitised and stored on a machine that's connected to the internet.

If you really need to take pornographic images of yourself, don't save those images to a cloud storage service. Don't save ANYTHING to a cloud storage service, unless you'd be comfortable with sharing it with the world.

Leaks tend to differ in magnitude and scale, too. Take, for example, the leak which affected Marks and Spencer[14]. This wasn't a malicious leak or the result of a hacker bypassing their security systems. In this case, a fault on their website allowed some customers to view each other's details. The company had to shut down its site for two hours whilst it dealt with the problem, leading to a huge loss in terms of potential earnings from online shoppers.

---

[14] See: http://www.bbc.co.uk/news/technology-34656818

Another great example of a minor leak is the one that affected British Gas and which led to the exposure of the e-mail addresses and passwords of 2,200 customers[15], although no bank or credit card details were compromised. British Gas quickly disabled the accounts and notified each of the customers who were affected.

Let's take a look at another quick case study.

Case Study: *Talk Talk Hack*
Classification: *Hacks and Leaks*

What Happened:

Up to 1.2 million e-mail addresses, names, phone numbers and bank details were accessed by a group of hackers in a cyberattack that took place towards the end of 2015. Talk Talk denied that this figure was accurate, and claimed that the hackers accessed 28,000 obscured credit and debit card details with the middle six digits removed, as well as 15,000 customer dates of birth.

Multiple suspects were eventually detained for the attack, including a sixteen-year-old boy from West London, a fifteen-year-old boy from Northern Ireland, and a twenty-year-old man from Staffordshire.

How it Could've Been Avoided:

TalkTalk responded in all of the right ways, although they are at fault to some extent for having a vulnerable website in the first place. In many cases, the perpetrators of hacks and leaks are never caught, which could suggest that in this case they were skilled amateurs without enough

---

[15] See: http://www.bbc.co.uk/news/technology-34663210

experience to hide their tracks.

For consumers who were affected by the attack, the official advice was to change all passwords, to beware of scammers attempting to contact them as fake representatives of TalkTalk, and to monitor bank accounts for suspicious activity. If your card details are ever used because of such a breach, you should report it to your bank and to the police.

With all of these high-profile hacks and leaks hitting the headlines, it's no surprise that people are paranoid. In fact, a whopping 44% of survey respondents are worried about being hacked, and almost a quarter (23.3%) of people said that one or more of their accounts has already been affected.

In all fairness, there are a lot of misunderstandings about hacks and leaks, as mentioned at the start of this chapter. If your partner knows your password and logs into your account without permission, for example, it's not a hack. It's unauthorised access.

Hacking requires an element of technical skill, and the people who do it deploy a variety of tools and techniques, including password cracking software, malware and security exploits. Guessing someone else's password usually requires you to know the name of their childhood pet or their date and place of birth.

Perhaps it's no coincidence, then, that the number of survey respondents who have fallen victim to a hack (23.3%) is virtually identical to the number of respondents that have shared their password with somebody else (23.1%). This is a big no-no if you want to stay safe and secure online.

Ideally, you should use different passwords for every website that you access, and you should never share your password under any circumstance. If possible, you should also use a minimum length of twelve to fourteen characters and include lowercase and uppercase letters, as well as numbers and symbols.

Creating a secure password for every single site can seem daunting. If you end up having to write your passwords down, then it makes the whole endeavour pointless. Personally, I use a long string of letters, characters, numbers and symbols, but I use the same password across all websites. I also change it on a regular basis for added security.

Option	Responses

One or more of my accounts has been hacked	23.32%
Someone has shared confidential information about me online	10.37%
One or more other people know my password	23.09%
I worry about being hacked	43.93%
I worry that companies will leak my information	46.76%

(Source: Survey)

Perhaps the most telling statistic of all is the fact that almost half of all survey respondents (46.8%) worry that companies will leak their information, and with good reason. Unfortunately, there's not a huge amount that you can do to combat this, except for sharing as little information as possible to begin with.

The good news is that there are laws in place to protect consumers. Despite the paranoia and the bad press, I believe that the vast majority of companies have their users' best interests at heart. But it only takes one bad apple to spoil the bunch, and there are plenty of bad apples on the internet.

Still, it might ease your paranoia to know that America and the United Kingdom, as well as the majority of the Western world, have strict laws on what brands are allowed to do with your data. For example, in the UK, you need to receive explicit permission from people before you send out e-mail marketing messages. It's also a requirement for the e-mails to include an unsubscribe option.

The problem is that not everyone obeys the law. A lot of spam, for example, is a direct result of automated bots that scour the internet for e-mail addresses. If you're ever unsure of the difference between legitimate and illegitimate messages, check for an unsubscribe link. If there's no unsubscribe link, then that company is breaking the law. So why would you buy from them?

Unfortunately, even if a company is following the rulebook, your data is still only as safe as their database is. If they store unencrypted information or if their security systems are vulnerable, it's easy for a hacker to access it.

Of course, a leak can be a PR disaster for any company, and brands are just as vulnerable as individuals. And let's be clear about this. A hack can be even more damaging than a leak, and they often have a real-world impact. Let's take a look at another case study.

Case Study: *Associated Press Hack*
Classification: *Hacks and Leaks*

What Happened:

The Associated Press is one of the most well-respected news organisations in the world. So when their Twitter account was hacked, all hell broke loose. The account was compromised in April of 2013, and a tweet was posted which claimed that the White House was under attack and that President Barack Obama had been injured.

The fake tweet caused a panic on Twitter and seriously affected the stock market with a 143-point fall in the Dow Jones industrial average. Fortunately, the tweet was corrected and the market quickly recovered, but it's a fantastic example of how social networking sites are starting to have a real impact on the world around us.

How it Could've Been Avoided:

A stronger password might have helped, but it depends upon how the hackers managed to gain access. Either way, the account could have been strengthened if it used two-factor authentication, which requires the user to log in using both their password and their mobile phone. It adds a couple of seconds to the login process, but it also keeps your account secure.

Two-factor authentication wasn't a feature on Twitter at the time, but it was rolled out shortly afterwards – potentially in response to the hack, although users had been calling for it for several years.

Either way, the Associated Press reacted well to the situation with AP employees correcting it almost immediately and issuing a swift apology at the start of the daily White House press briefing. They also suspended all of their Twitter accounts until they could be checked for security to stop the same thing from happening again.

Not all hacks cause such tangible damage, but they can still cause a lot of trouble and embarrassment, both for brands and for consumers. However, it often works the other way around. For example, if an obscure brand gets hacked and the news goes viral, it's possible that they'll see a spike in sales. A lot depends upon the reputation of the brand and the severity of the hack.

A cynic might also argue that we're too trusting. In fact, brands have faked hacks on their own accounts to generate publicity. MTV is a great example of this. In February of 2013, the music company was "hacked" by its rivals at Black Entertainment Television.

However, Annie Shoening, the marketing director of MTV US, tweeted about the hack before it actually took place, and the company eventually revealed that it was a publicity stunt saying: "We totally catfished you guys. Thanks for playing."

We'll talk more about catfishing later on, but in the meantime, let's take a quick look at the infamous Burger King hack, which I wrote about for The Drum[16].

Case Study: *Burger King Hack*
Classification: *Hacks and Leaks*

What Happened:

---

[16] See: http://www.thedrum.com/opinion/2013/02/19/burger-king-twitter-hack-can-fast-food-giant-capitalise-its-sudden-exposure

Burger King's verified Twitter account was compromised by a hacker who was able to update the imagery and profile copy to refer to McDonald's and to tweet a series of links to YouTube videos.

Despite the fact that the compromised account posted numerous tweets in support of McDonald's, an official spokesman for the rival company said, "We empathise with our @BurgerKing counterparts. Rest assured, we had nothing to do with the hacking."

Burger King eventually reclaimed the account after an hour and a half. By then, they'd picked up 30,000 new followers and over 2,000 retweets.

How it Could've Been Avoided:

It could be argued that the company's community managers should have responded more quickly, but it can be difficult to work under pressure and if no plan's in place to limit potential damage then it can take time just to figure out what's happening.

Unfortunately, the hack took place before Twitter launched two-factor authentication, which is a fantastic way to protect your account. If we assume that Burger King's employees were using secure passwords and up-to-date antivirus software, there's not much more that they could have done.

That said, Burger King failed to capitalise on the publicity that the attack helped to generate, and it would have been a good idea for the company to have posted an official response. An apology would also have gone a long way, even though they weren't, strictly speaking, at fault.

As these case studies show, it's a minefield out there. Your social networking accounts could be more vulnerable than you think, and you'd be surprised at the amount of damage that an unauthorised user can cause.

This brings us on to the topic of "fraping," when a friend or family member gains unauthorised access to your Facebook page in order to post a bogus update. Typically, they're able to access your account because you left yourself logged into a computer or because you left your phone unattended.

Most people see fraping as harmless fun, but that's not always the case. Fraping can also cause concerns from a security point of view. If you work in marketing, like 10% of our survey respondents, then it's likely that your Facebook account is hooked up to the pages that you manage. And if someone is able to frape you then they have unrestricted access to your account, which means that they could post from your company pages, too.

TOP DEFINITION

Frape

A combination of the words 'Facebook' and 'Rape'.

The act of Raping someones Facebook profile when they leave it logged in. Profile pictures, sexuality and interests are commonly changed however fraping can include the poking or messaging of strangers from someone else's Facebook account.

Dude, did you see Jonny's Facebook profile, someone fraped him big time.

by Phaliure June 12, 2007

(Source: UrbanDictionary.com)

So what can you do to protect yourself against hacks and leaks? Well, whilst you can't make yourself immune to them, there are still several steps to take.

Two-Factor Authentication:

Two-factor authentication is used to identify users by asking them to provide two different forms of ID. A great example of this is the humble cash machine, which requires the combination of a debit card and a pin number. Even if someone had access to one of them, they'd still need the other to take any money out. In social networking terms, two-factor authentication typically refers to a login system that requires you to provide a password and then to enter a code from an automated SMS message.

Always Log Out:

This one's a no-brainer, particularly if you use public machines. Ideally, you should log out of every website at the end of each of your browsing sessions, although this isn't always practical. And it goes without saying that you shouldn't allow your browser to remember your password.

Use Secure Passwords:

As a general rule, your password becomes more secure if you avoid real words and stick to a random combination of letters and numbers. Use a minimum of ten characters, and create a different password for each website if possible. Following these precautions will make it harder for people to guess your passwords, and it'll also make it harder for computer programmers to figure them out by running through different algorithms.

Keep it Secret:

Again, this tip is an obvious one, but you'd be surprised at how many people fail to follow it. Avoid sharing your password with anyone. If you ever feel the need to do so, immediately change all of your passwords afterwards to strengthen your accounts.

Password Protect Your Phone:

Unprotected phones are, anecdotally at least, one of the most common causes of frapes and unauthorised access. Be sure to use passwords or passcodes on your mobile devices and to opt for fingerprint recognition when possible. Again, a good hacker could bypass these security measures, but they'd have to have a lot of skill and a lot of time to do so.

Use Up-to-Date Antivirus Software:

Using antivirus software is all well and good, but if you don't keep it up-to-date then it isn't going to be as effective. If your computer is connected to the internet, you should have real-time antivirus software installed to stop threats before they become a problem. I'm not going to go into the differences between the different types of viruses, but they're all pretty nasty and it's easily possible for a virus to compromise your accounts' security.

Be Careful When Clicking Links:

If a friend sends you a link that looks suspicious, double-check with them before you click on it. Remember, most link-based viruses work by compromising the security of your account and then forwarding the same virus on to your contacts.

CHAPTER FOUR: MISUNDERSTANDINGS

THE INTERNET CAN BE a confusing place. Just ask any of your elderly relatives. Even for digital natives – people who were born and raised in the age of the internet and who don't remember a time before broadband – there can be a lot to take in.

It was bad enough in the early days of the internet, when you only had to worry about IRC commands and e-mail spam. Nowadays, with the rise of social networking and user-generated content, it's easier than ever to feel confused or overwhelmed.

That's why it's so important to avoid ambiguity when you're using social networking sites. When you're interacting with people online, you're unable to pick up on things such as body language, pacing and tonality, which we usually use as a sort of subconscious indicator of a person's true intent.

In a 2007 article for the New York Times[17], psychologist Dr. Daniel Goleman explained, "In contrast to a phone call or talking in person, e-mail can be emotionally impoverished when it comes to nonverbal messages that add nuance and valence to our words. The typed words are denuded of the rich emotional context we convey in person or over the phone."

Interestingly enough, Goleman continues to talk about how we tend to see positive e-mail messages as more neutral and neutral ones as more negative than the sender intended. He also explains that familiarity between the sender and receiver can help to reduce the number of misunderstandings.

The same article also included comments from Clay Shirky, a professor in New York University's interactive telecommunications programme. Shirky specialises in social computing, software programmes through which

---

[17] See: http://www.nytimes.com/2007/10/07/jobs/07pre.html

multiple users interact.

"When you communicate with a group you only know through electronic channels," Shirky says, "it's like having functional Asperger's Syndrome. You are very logical and rational but emotionally brittle."

As the article was written in 2007, most of today's social networking sites were yet to be created, but it's easy to see how Shirky's insights were ahead of their time. If it's easy to misunderstand people via e-mail, then it follows that the fast-paced world of social networking has the potential to be even more difficult to navigate.

Despite this, a surprisingly high percentage (52.4%) of survey respondents said that they find it easy to communicate on social networking sites. This could be for a number of reasons. For example, if you only use one site to interact with friends and family with whom you've already built up a rapport, then you're going to find it easier to communicate than if you use a dozen social networking sites to interact with the general public, as is the case for marketers.

Anecdotally, it's also clear to me that some people are better at online communication than others. Using emoticons can help people to understand your meaning. It also helps if you write using correct spelling and grammar, regardless of the language that you're using.

In fact, spelling and grammar mistakes cost companies millions, whether we're talking about the cash that Scope splashed to promote a tweet that didn't make grammatical sense, or whether we're talking about a typo in the description of an expensive product on a shopping site.

ScopeMouthwash
@ScopeMouthwash

Where there's a bottle of Scope, there's a way. RT if your planning a fresh NYE kiss. #ScopeKiss

Promoted by ScopeMouthwash

12/28/12, 6:38 PM

166 RETWEETS **45** FAVORITES

(Source: Twitter.com)

According to online entrepreneur Charles Duncombe, an analysis of website figures shows that a single spelling mistake can cut online sales in half[18]. He also notes that "when you sell or communicate on the internet, 99% of the time it is done with the written word."

Duncombe's analysis was based upon the average revenue per visitor on TightsPlease.co.uk, with revenue doubling after errors were corrected. He believes that spelling is important to the credibility of a website, although he does note that in some more informal parts of the internet, such as on social networking sites, there's a greater tolerance for poor spelling and grammar.

In the end, social networking is all about communication, and anything that hampers this communication can have adverse effects. Likewise, anything that enhances it can make it easier for you to communicate with your friends and followers, which is why we use emoticons.

emoticon

A simple text depiction of what one's face would look like if an online conversation were taking place in person.

1. I'm happy! :)

2. I'm unhappy! :(

3. You're silly! :P

by PJC October 01, 2002

(Source: UrbanDictionary.com)

---

[18] See: http://www.bbc.co.uk/news/education-14130854

Emoticons are useful because they act as a visual clue. In fact, a 2014 study in the journal *Social Neuroscience*[19] found that looking at emoticons can trigger the same facial recognition response in the occipitotemporal parts of the brain that we experience when we look at the faces of other human beings. But they won't help you to work miracles.

Perhaps it's no surprise then that 38.3% of survey respondents said that they sometimes feel confused by other people's updates. To understand this, it can help to go back to the very roots of communication. All communication is comprised of a sender and a receiver. The sender has a message that they want to transmit, and they try to deliver their message as clearly as possible, but the meaning can be lost along the way.

This could happen due to any of a number of reasons, from the recipient mishearing the message to uncertainty on the part of a sender. One common example, which happens fairly often on social networking sites, is when two people are involved in a conflict or an argument and they each assume that the other person is going to be hostile. In this instance, any ambiguous message will be interpreted as hostile, even if the intent was never there on the part of the sender.

Misunderstandings can also occur due to ignorance on the part of the user, which is what happened in our next case study.

Case Study: *Ed Balls*
Classification: *Misunderstanding*

What Happened:

On April 28th 2011, British politician Ed Balls posted a tweet which simply

---

[19] See: http://www.wired.com/2014/02/brain-smiley-emoticon-science/

read, "Ed Balls." It later emerged that he'd been attempting a vanity search[20], but that he'd misunderstood how to use Twitter.

Balls's gaffe has accumulated over 55,000 retweets and 28,000 likes at the time of writing, and it has turned him into a meme. Major publications such as The Telegraph have even released round-ups of Ed Balls Day, which denizens of the internet celebrate every year on the anniversary of the original tweet.

How it Could've Been Avoided:

Ed Balls could have avoided the mistake by familiarising himself with how Twitter worked before using it, and the "damage" could have been limited if he'd been quick to delete the post.

However, in a rare moment of digital savvy, Balls has taken the mistake in his stride. Even if he is a little bemused about the publicity that it created, he still participates in Ed Balls Day celebrations each year to the delight of the tens of thousands of people who mark the occasion.

As the above example demonstrates, not all misunderstandings lead to problems. In fact, they can often be entertaining. But conflict on social networking sites may be more common than you think, with 33% of survey respondents admitting to arguing with people over social media.

Jokes and humorous status updates can also lead to confusion, particularly if people don't understand the joke .In fact, 23% of survey respondents say that they've made a joke on social media that has been taken the wrong way.

---

[20] A search for your own name.

According to a report in *The Atlantic*[21], most people suffer from a phenomenon called "the transparency illusion," a belief that their intentions are crystal clear to others despite the fact that they haven't necessarily communicated them.

Even if you are communicating clearly, you can still run into problems if the receiver isn't being receptive. People need to feel good about themselves if they want to function well, but this can lead to complications. If someone's sense of self is threatened, such as if they interact with someone who's better at a job that they both share, then this need for positive reinforcement can lead them to judge the other person more harshly.

One study by Maria Agthe, Matthias Spörrle and Jon K. Maner[22] found that during the interview stage, attractive job applicants were judged as less qualified by members of the same sex than they were by members of the opposite sex, suggesting that jealousy was at play.

Transmitting clear signals to others could have further benefits, too. Researchers have found[23] that people who send clear signals are more satisfied with their relationships, careers and lives than people who are difficult to read.

Of course, being clear about your intentions is something that can affect brands just as much as consumers. Let's take a look at a quick case study.

Case Study: *Give a Child a Breakfast Fail*
Classification: *Misunderstanding*

What Happened:

It all began after Kellogg's commissioned the Lost Education report, which aimed to look into hunger in the classroom. The report had some surprising

---

[21] See: http://www.theatlantic.com/health/archive/2015/04/mixed-signals-why-people-misunderstand-each-other/391053/

[22] See: http://psp.sagepub.com/content/37/8/1042.abstract

[23] See: http://www.ncbi.nlm.nih.gov/pubmed/23861354

findings - such as the fact that children arriving at school hungry miss out on the equivalent of 70% of a school term throughout their primary school career[24]. So Kellogg's launched its Give a Child a Breakfast campaign with the aim of giving away two million breakfasts to 1,000 breakfast clubs.

The problem is, they didn't think it through. The company created a campaign video and told their followers that each watch, share or retweet of the campaign video equalled one breakfast. Unfortunately, the reaction from the general public was mixed with one person asking, "Is [the] message, 'Retweet us or children will go hungry?'"

How it Could've Been Avoided:

Whilst Kellogg's had their heart in the right place, someone on their digital marketing team should have realised that there was the potential for a backlash. Charitable initiatives usually do well on social, but people are quick to spot when you're doing something with an ulterior motive.

Kellogg's had already been funding breakfast clubs for over fifteen years, so it's understandable that they received a mixed reaction. In the past, Kellogg's simply funded the meals. By requiring people to share their campaign video, they implied that funding would actually be withdrawn if they didn't reach their target.

Fortunately, the company quickly apologised, but the damage had already been done. In this instance, the blame can be placed at the feet of whoever organised the campaign without considering what the response might be from the public.

---

[24] See: http://pressoffice.kelloggs.co.uk/index.php?s=20295&item=122412

As this chapter has taught you, misunderstandings are a product of human error. Whilst brands can be vulnerable to them, it's inevitably because somebody, somewhere, made a mistake.

Luckily, knowing is half the battle. Now that you're aware of the potential for misunderstandings on social networking sites, you can try to avoid them with the following tips and tricks.

Read Your Post Aloud:

The simple act of reading your post aloud can often be enough to make you realise that there are mistakes or hidden meanings. You'd be surprised at how often miscommunication occurs simply because someone forgot to sense-check.

Use Emoticons:

As discussed earlier in this chapter, emoticons have the same effect on our brains as real faces. By using emoticons in your posts, you can increase the likelihood that your meaning will still be intact by the time that your message reaches its recipient.

Check Spelling/Grammar:

Spelling and grammar mistakes can completely change the meaning of a sentence. Even when they don't, they're bound to annoy pedants like myself. I usually find that a single spelling mistake is enough to make me stop reading – so much for miscommunication. It's not miscommunication if your bad grammar stops the recipient from processing the message in the first place.

Elaborate:

Unless you're on a site like Twitter, where your messages are limited to 140 characters, you have enough space to elaborate. For example, don't post an update to say, "I can't believe it." Instead, avoid confusion and misunderstandings by elaborating: "I can't believe my new dress arrived when I only ordered it this morning."

Wear the Other Person's Shoes

This might sound like a cliché, but try to put yourself in the other person's shoes. If you're sending a message to someone, consider how they're likely to react to it before you hit the send button. This will help you to avoid embarrassment, because, let's face it, we all put our foot in it sometimes.

If in Doubt, Don't Post:

Sometimes, the best option is just to refrain from saying anything at all. Alternatively, don't use social media. Pick up the phone and give someone a call instead. Even when you speak on the phone, you pick up on verbal cues and pauses that aren't available if you're conversing via text over the internet.

CHAPTER FIVE: VIRALITY

AH, VIRALITY. It's the holy grail of digital marketing or a massive pain in the backside, depending upon your point of view. When we talk about virality, we're talking about the way in which a piece of content can be shared from person-to-person in real-time to such an extent that it's seen by thousands or even millions of people over a short space of time.

Of course, this means that brands and companies have jumped on the bandwagon, and marketers are under pressure from their CEOs to create the next viral video. Unfortunately, it's not that easy. No one really knows what will capture the world's attention, and it always seems to be the most unlikely things that end up notching up millions of shares or views.

Virality is a natural side effect of social networking, and it's been happening since way before the internet. Back in the day, you'd tell two friends about a book, and then they'd both tell two friends, and so on and so on until it became a bestseller.

But the internet has democratised sharing. Now, if you have a book recommendation, you can quickly share it with your Facebook and Twitter followers, or you could write about it on your blog so that your thoughts are preserved for posterity.

Sharing is powerful, and it can build and destroy careers in a heartbeat. Let's take a look at how virality was enough to guarantee a global hit for an obscure Korean popstar.

Case Study: *Psy Breaks YouTube*
Classification: *Virality*

What Happened:

On July 15th 2012, South Korean musician Psy released the music video for his new single, "Gangnam Style." Against all the odds, the video caught the public's imagination, and it was rapidly shared and disseminated. "Gangnam Style" became the first YouTube video to hit one billion views; at the time of writing, it's up to 2.6 billion views and is the most popular video on the site.

The song eventually crossed over into mainstream culture, and it became common to hear it on radio stations and TV shows. It also topped the charts in over thirty countries, and Psy's bizarre dance moves became a phenomenon.

How it Could Be Repeated:

This case study was selected to show the power of viral sharing and not because it illustrates a mistake. That said, we can pinpoint a few of the factors that caught the public's imagination. His wacky dress sense and dance moves, for example. For Psy, all of the factors came together at the right time, and that's what made his video a success.

Psy's case study illustrates an interesting quandary. Are viral videos a good thing or a bad thing? After all, they provide joy and entertainment for millions, but they can also seriously affect the lives of the people who star in them, as is the case with Star Wars Kid, who we discussed in the introduction and who we'll take a closer look at later on in this chapter.

Virality is a double-edged sword. If a photo of you goes viral, then you're going to be subjected to intense public scrutiny. Some people thrive on the attention and others despise it. In fact, the vast majority of people would prefer to avoid it with just 20.4% of survey respondents saying that they'd feel comfortable if a picture or video of them went viral.

And it turns out that most people have a cynical opinion of viral videos, with over half (54.6%) of respondents believing that most viral videos are at the expense of the originator. It's certainly true that the proliferation of smartphones has led to a culture in which you could be filmed at any time. And if you are being secretly filmed, there's not a huge amount that you can do about it once the video has been shared and disseminated online.

Likewise, our survey respondents have a bleak view of the potential repercussions of going viral with less than a third of people (32.2%) believing that they'd keep their job if they appeared in a viral video.

It's true that people have lost their jobs after going viral, but it's also true that some of them deserved it. The most common mistake that people make is to rant about their colleagues or their customers. Business Insider released an article in 2011[25] listing seventeen times people were fired for using Facebook, including thirteen Virgin Airlines crew members who were fired after publicly discussing faulty engines and cockroach infestations in the cabins.

Perhaps that's one of the reasons why only 13.1% of respondents believe that viral videos are a good thing. That result surprised me because it seems as though almost everyone loves to watch and share the latest video. Or maybe people remember what happened to Star Wars Kid.

Case Study: *Star Wars Kid*
Classification: *Virality*

What Happened:

In 2002, Ghyslain Raza used an 8mm video camera to film himself swinging a golf ball retriever like a lightsaber. The video was never intended for public release, but a friend found the cassette and uploaded it to the internet. It gained some popularity through peer-to-peer file sharing

---

[25] See: http://www.businessinsider.com/facebook-fired-2011-5

services, but it really took off in 2006 after it was uploaded to YouTube.

Raza has since claimed to be a victim of cyberbullying due to the negative attention that the video received. One person described him as "a pox on humanity," whilst others tried to goad him into committing suicide.

How it Could've Been Avoided:

This case study highlights the fact that once something is digital, it's difficult to get rid of. Raza could have avoided all of the attention by storing his initial video more securely. As soon as his friend found it and digitised it, he was no longer in control of it.

That said, Star Wars Kid highlights the darker side of humanity, which can often be observed in the comments on YouTube. Fortunately, there were also plenty of positive comments, with one group of Star Wars enthusiasts saying, "That's why his video was so popular. It was funny and awkward, but ultimately, we connected with him."

Raza will have to live with being Star Wars Kid for the rest of his life, but by focusing on the positives and ignoring the negatives, he can at least improve his outlook. He's also done a great job of damage control by turning the negativity of cyberbullying into the positivity of being an activist.

Star Wars Kid has gone on to become a meme in his own right, a rare honour. Memes are slightly different to viral videos, although they're caused by similar phenomena. If you've spent any time on the internet, you've probably seem a meme. The most recognisable memes are effectively just images with text overlaid on top of them.

Most internet memes have a specific meaning. Take, for example, Grumpy Cat. You've probably seen a photo of her doing the rounds, alongside a caption which plays upon the fact that the cat looks so miserable. Another example is Bad Luck Brian, which is fairly self-explanatory. It's a photo of a geeky-looking high school kid, and it's always captioned with something unfortunate, such as: "Rides bumper cars. Killed by drunk driver."

The term meme was coined by evolutionary biologist Richard Dawkins in his seminal 1976 release, *The Selfish Gene*. Broadly speaking, a meme is an idea, a style or a behaviour which spreads from person-to-person within a culture. Dawkins used it to explain cultural phenomena such as melodies, catchphrases and fashion trends.

When Dawkins first coined the term, the internet was in its formative years. Tim Berners Lee didn't invent the World Wide Web until 1989. But it's easy to see how its usage has evolved over time.

TOP DEFINITION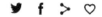

Memeophobia 🔊

A distinct, 21st century fear that a photograph or video posted on a social network medium will go viral and you will forever be immortalized in internet infamy.

Anthony, don't post that picture, you know I have memeophobia! I'm afraid to become a meme!

by sunsetblvd March 30, 2015

(Source: UrbanDictionary.com)

Memes are now so widespread that sites like UrbanDictionary.com, which lists slang and derivative words that are in common usage but that aren't listed by regular dictionaries, are full of spin-offs of the term, including "memeophobia." Memeophobia is interesting because it ties in with our survey responses. Only 20.4% of people would feel comfortable if a photo of them went viral.

And there's good reason for this, too. Take, for example, the case of Heidi Yeh, a Taiwanese model who became an internet meme after a fake news story about her went viral[26]. According to Yeh, the article led to the breakdown of her relationship and the loss of approximately £80,000 in earnings. She told reporters, "I've broken down many times crying and haven't been able to sleep."

Option	Responses
I'd feel comfortable if a photo or video of me went viral	20.36%
I think that most viral videos are at the expensive of the originator	54.60%
If I appeared in a viral video doing a stupid dance, I think I'd keep my job	32.17%
Viral videos are a good thing	13.10%

(Source: Survey)

I discovered a related term in a book called *That Should be a Word.* by Lizzie Skurnick. Skurnick's book focuses on words that don't exist but that should do, and one of her terms was sharanoia.

Sharanoia
(SHARE-uh-NOY—uh), n.
Fear of what people are thinking of your posts.

"Even though she had only seventy-two friends, Irina suffered from such sharanoia that she often deleted her updates before people even responded."

---

[26] See: http://www.bbc.co.uk/news/world-asia-34568674

(Source: Lizzie Skurnick - That Should be a Word)

As we've discovered in this chapter, it's all too easy to be affected by memes and viral videos, and so perhaps you're right to be sharanoid. Fortunately, there are a few things that you can do to keep yourself safe.

Privacy Settings:

It's a given that you should familiarise yourself with the privacy settings on your social networks of choice, but this is particularly important if you want to avoid people sharing your content.

Limit Tagging Capabilities:

Many social networks allow you to manually approve any tags that people use, so that you're notified before anything appears on your profile. This is particularly useful if you hate being photographed.

Don't Upload Old Photos:

Old photos can be incredibly embarrassing, both for yourself and for your family and friends. If you must upload old photos, consider who's likely to view them, and be sure to check with your friends before you upload them to save embarrassment. If you do become a meme, you don't want it to be because of your old high school yearbook photo.

Consider Takedown Requests:

Most social networks will allow you to report other users for copyright infringement. Unfortunately, these reports often take time to get processed, if they're acted on at all. Once your content is online, it's pretty much impossible to remove it if people decide to share it. Use this as a last resort only.

CHAPTER SIX: LEGACY

THIS CHAPTER DEALS with your legacy and how your social networking activity could easily outlive you. Some social networks have even introduced special features to deal with death. On Facebook, for example, a profile can be memorialised, which leaves it intact but prohibits any future activity.

Because of the fleeting nature of social networking sites and the speed with which we can post things, we often forget about their permanence. Just because you've forgotten about something, it doesn't mean it's gone for good. If you don't believe me, download the archive of your activity on a social networking site[27] and see how easy it is to go through years of updates.

The word legacy has two different meanings when it comes to social networking. The first and most recognisable usage refers to the actual legacy that we'll leave behind when we're dead and buried. The second usage refers to posts from a long time ago. For example, "legacy posts" are posts from several years ago that you've long since forgotten.

Perhaps unsurprisingly, over three-quarters of our survey respondents admitted googling their name to see what comes up. In fact, there's even a term for it – "vanity searching." Back in the day, it used to be looked down upon because it implied that you had an ego. Nowadays, with the proliferation of internet access, it makes perfect sense. After all, you could be googled by anyone from potential employers to friends and family members. It's important to familiarise yourself with what they're likely to see.

But what should you do if something negative appears? Well, that's a good question. Google's algorithms are incredibly complicated and beyond the scope of this book, but suffice to say that you don't get much of a say about which results appear.

---

[27] Many social networks will allow you to download an archive containing all of the updates that you've posted since joining the service.

Still, you have options. Certain authoritative websites tend to outrank others, so you could sign up to social networking sites en masse to try to displace the existing results. The other option is to file a right to be forgotten request. Let's take a quick look at that.

Case Study: *Right to be Forgotten*
Classification: *Legacy*

What Happened:

The right to be forgotten is a concept that was discussed and deployed by the European Union, which argues that everyone has a human right to be "forgotten" when it comes to the access of information. In practice, that means that if there's a news article which names you as the victim of a crime, for example, and you don't want that information to be public, search engines should adhere to your requests and block the content when other users search for it.

Because of this, major search engines have been forced to adapt their operating policies to comply with the new regulations, which outlined thirteen pieces of criteria that companies must consider when evaluating whether to honour a request[28].. By October 2014, Google alone had received over 140,000 requests with approximately 60% of those requests being honoured[29].

---

[28] See: http://searchengineland.com/eu-issues-right-forgotten-criteria-209880

[29] See: http://www.wired.co.uk/news/archive/2014-10/10/google-right-to-be-forgotten-transparency

How it Could've Been Avoided:

For starters, the courts have placed responsibility in the wrong hands. Search engines simply list results, and removing a result won't remove the content from the site that it's featured on. However, forcing each of these websites to comply would be impossible, and so search engines are forced to do the dirty work.

The best way to avoid right to be forgotten requests is to avoid negativity in the first place. Unfortunately, the right to be forgotten ruling has had all sorts of ethical implications, including the fact that criminals could find it easier to hide their pasts.

Interestingly enough, despite the fact that most people have carried out a vanity search, barely a third (36.4%) of respondents can remember which results appeared. This may be because of the way that search engine results pages tend to change over time. The results for a search in February are often totally different to the results for the same search in July.

Luckily, some people have already thought about their legacy, with 36.4% of respondents agreeing that they'd be comfortable if their statuses resurfaced in ten years' time. A further 39.2% of respondents claimed to have no regrets about their online activity.

But whatever people say, there's usually an outcry whenever a social network makes it easier for people to view their legacy posts. For example, when Facebook introduced timelines, there was a revolt from the general public because it became much, much easier to view old updates. But those same updates were visible beforehand. They just took more time to access. The same problem occurs with Facebook's "On This Day" feature, or with apps like Timehop that resurface old updates.

Option	Responses
I've Googled my name to see what comes up	76.25%
I know what results come up if you Google me	36.77%
I'd feel comfortable if my statuses from today were viewed in 2025	36.44%
I have no regrets about my online activity	39.15%

(Source: Survey)

This said, it's easy for you, as a user, to control what people can see. It just takes time, and people are lazy. Personally, I don't think there's anything wrong with leaving your old updates online, as long as you haven't done anything stupid. In the end, it comes down to personal choice.

One of the interesting things about your digital legacy is that, in many cases, it's made up of old profiles on social networking sites that you no longer use. These days, you don't just have to worry about Facebook because your Bebo or Myspace accounts could come back to haunt you, too.

But the problem is, at what point do you stop using a social network? It's not uncommon for people to leave a network multiple times, only to come back each time and to reclaim control of their account. In other cases, people simply forget that they signed up and just never log in again. Either way, it's a good idea to do a regular audit (by carrying out a vanity search) and to delete your profiles from any websites that you don't intend to use again. In most cases, this will delete your data, too.

Case Study: *Tom Hardy's Old Photos Myspace*
Classification: *Legacy*

What Happened:

Tom Hardy is a British actor who made his debut in *Black Hawk Down* and who later starred in *The Dark Knight Rises*, *Mad Max: Fury Road*, and numerous other films and TV shows. In 2015, several major news outlets published old photos from Hardy's Myspace page. There was nothing incendiary, but they did portray the actor in a different light.

Hardy went on record to say that he wasn't ashamed of the photos, and whilst they trended several times on major social networking sites, there were no real upsets or controversies.

How it Could've Been Avoided:

This one is pretty easy. Hardy could have avoided the situation by not uploading the photos to his Myspace page in the first place. He could also have logged into the account and deleted the images, especially after his fame began to accelerate. Once the images were republished, however, they were no longer under his control.

They say there's no such thing as bad publicity. By responding in an authentic, human way, Hardy affirmed that he had nothing to be ashamed of, earning respect from fans and non-fans alike.

The main problem for anyone who's concerned about their legacy is the amount of data that's out there and the fact that it's all interlinked. It's easy to look like an idiot after using Spotify, for example, because your Facebook friends can see you listening to your guilty pleasures. Likewise, your old posts are archived and indexed by social networking sites and search engines, and so people can still stumble across them.

You've probably witnessed this in action, if a friend has liked a status or a post from several years ago. Likewise, it's easy to find yourself doing the same thing if you're browsing at random from link to link. Or if you're "stalking" people on Facebook.

When people talk about Facebook stalking, they're usually referring to the act of using the network to find information on specific people, often by browsing through their legacy posts. Common examples include a guy who spends his evenings looking at his ex-girlfriend's profile or a One Direction fan who keeps going through the band's old updates.

TOP DEFINITION

facebook stalking

A covert method of investigation using **facebook**.com. Good for discovering a wealth of information about people you don't actually know.

person 1: Did you go to the _____ party last night?
person 2: No, but I was routinely facebook stalking (insert name of person you have never actually spoken to but have frequently visited his/her facebook profile)'s photos and saw pictures from it. It looked fetch.

by Jenny19 December 27, 2005

(Source: UrbanDictionary.com)

Cyberstalking is much more serious, the online equivalent of traditional stalking. There are a number of laws and regulations which govern cyberstalking, depending upon the region that you're in, but they can be difficult for authorities to act upon.

Cyberstalking is more common than you might realise. In fact, as far back as April 2011, The Guardian reported[30] that cyberstalking is now more common than offline stalking. They also revealed that nearly 40% of cyberstalking victims are male, a figure which stands at 20% for offline stalking. On top of this, the majority of people knew their stalkers, despite only 4% of them being former partners (compared to half for offline stalkers).

When it comes to Facebook stalking, people are far more open and it's considered by most to be a part of life on the social network. One infographic from 2012[31] revealed some surprising statistics. A survey of American college students found that 83% of them regularly checked an ex's profile, 74% of them checked the profile of their ex's new partner, and 70% used a friend's account to check a profile after being unfriended.

TOP DEFINITION

cyberstalking

Cyberstalking, which is simply an extension of the physical form of stalking, is where the electronic mediums such as the Internet are used to pursue, harass or contact another in an unsolicited fashion. Most often, given the vast distances that the Internet spans, this behaviour will never manifest itself in the physical sense but this does not mean that the pursuit is any less distressing. There are a wide variety of means by which individuals may seek out and harass individuals even though they may not share the same geographic borders, and this may present a range of physical, emotional, and psychological consequences to the victim.

Person A: "Did you hear about Alfonse, hes totally cyberstalking this chick from another country"

by batgimp January 19, 2007

---

[30] See: http://www.theguardian.com/uk/2011/apr/08/cyberstalking-study-victims-men

[31] See: http://ansonalex.com/infographics/facebook-stalking-statistics-2012-infographic/

(Source: UrbanDictionary.com)

Facebook is also commonly used to check on current partners, and people often have something to hide. Even in 2009, when Facebook was less popular than it is in the present day, it was cited in 20% of American divorce papers[32].

But have no fear. There are steps you can take to protect your legacy, and they'll help you to stop Facebook stalkers, too. After all, if you've removed everything that could cause embarrassment, then does it matter who's looking at your updates?

We'll dedicate the rest of this chapter to safeguarding your legacy before moving on to look at privacy.

Vanity Searches:

We've already talked about vanity searches. They can be a great way to see what other people might see if they search for you. Consider running a vanity search and digging through the first ten pages of results to see what shows up. You might be surprised! If you do find something questionable, contact the webmaster to ask them to remove it.

Shutting Down Profiles:

Is your old Myspace account still online? What about Bebo? Perhaps you're still a member on the forums you used to visit. Whatever the case, there's usually an option to delete your profile and all of the posts that are tied to it. Use this as a last resort because shutting down your profile will delete the good memories, as well as the bad.

Content Audits:

It's a good idea to flick through your old profiles once a year or so, just to

---

[32] See: http://www.ibtimes.com/study-1-5-divorces-us-caused-facebook-355172

see what's visible. Feelings, attitudes and situations tend to change over time, and so you might find that something that seemed innocuous could now cause problems. Regular content audits help you to identify what other people might be able to see; if you don't want them to see something, delete it.

Right to be Forgotten:

If you live within the European Union, you're covered by new legislation. Accordingly, if there's something showing up in search results that could damage your reputation, you can contact Google (and other search engines) to ask for the link to be removed. Right to be forgotten requests should only be used as a last resort.

Privacy Settings:

Most social networks allow you to specify who can see your profile and your updates. Facebook even allows you to backdate your settings. Tightening up your privacy settings can help to make sure that your legacy posts aren't visible to the general public.

CHAPTER SEVEN: PRIVACY

PRIVACY IS A HOT TOPIC, and it's one that affects us all. Updating your privacy settings can make a huge difference if you're trying to avoid a faux pas, and just knowing that your settings are correct can be enough to drive your paranoia away for good.

Many social media professionals assume that people are unaware of their options when it comes to privacy, but if our survey respondents are to be believed then that reputation is undeserved. A massive 86.7% of people said that they know how to change their privacy settings, and yet despite that, only 23% felt protected as a consequence.

This isn't a huge surprise. After all, it's a classic example of paranoia, and it ties in with the results of a 2014 report from TRUSTe[33], a company which specialises in privacy compliance. They found that a whopping 89% of British internet users are concerned about their online privacy with over a third of respondents claiming to "frequently" or "always" have concerns.

Option	Responses
I know how to change my privacy settings	86.75%
People have seen things that I didn't want them to see	10.93%
I feel protected by my privacy settings	22.96%
I trust social networks to keep my information secure	9.49%

(Source: Survey)

---

[33] See: https://econsultancy.com/blog/64209-89-of-british-internet-users-are-worried-about-online-privacy-report/

Interestingly, whilst online shopping caused the most concern – with 88% of consumers worrying about their privacy whilst shopping – social networking was close on its tail with 86%. This is despite the fact that the majority of people know how to change their privacy settings to protect themselves.

Admittedly, people don't always trust that their settings will protect them. In fact, just 9.5% of respondents said that they trust social networks to keep their information secure, even though only 11% of people have accidentally shared updates that they didn't want other people to see.

Perhaps this disparity is due to a lack of education. After all, most people use social networks for fun and have neither the time nor the inclination to find out how their data is being used. It's not uncommon for people to get upset over nothing, as our next case study demonstrates.

Case Study: *People Aren't Stealing Your Facebook Photos*
Classification: *Privacy*

What Happened:

Back in 2013, I wrote an article for Adweek[34] about a rumour that was sweeping through Facebook. A number of people believed that someone was stealing photos of their children and posting them to a page called Infancy. As a result, they banded together and started protesting with some updates receiving thousands of shares.

What they didn't realise was that Infancy was an automatically generated page that simply pulled in all of the photos and updates that users had access to on the topic of babies, infancy and childhood. In fact, users were unable to see anything that they couldn't have seen anywhere else.

[34] See: http://www.adweek.com/socialtimes/people-arent-stealing-your-facebook-photos-a-lesson-in-privacy/421081

How it Could've Been Avoided:

You could argue that Facebook should have done a better job of educating its users, but it's hard to lay blame at their feet. There are millions upon millions of these automatically generated pages, and in most cases, they come in useful.

As it stands, the issue lies with the users. Part of it is due to a lack of education, and part of it is due to them uploading photos of their children in the first place. Unfortunately, people love to get angry about privacy breaches, even when there wasn't a breach in the first place.

We've already talked about how difficult it is to remove a photo from the internet once someone has made a copy of it. Photos and videos are bad enough, but what happens when people share sensitive information?

In chapter two, we talked about the Boswell family, who were wrongly targeted in a backlash against some comments that were posted about the tragic death of a young child. Some Facebook users began sharing what was ostensibly the address of the person who made the comments, but the information was incorrect. As a result, the Boswells were wrongly targeted by real-life vigilantes who arrived at their door after acting on the false information.

The phenomenon of people researching and broadcasting personally identifiable information is called doxing, which comes from an altered abbreviation of the word "documents." In sharp contrast to hacking, which requires a certain amount of knowledge and skill, doxing is relatively straightforward.

doxing

Doxing is a technique of tracing someone or gather information about an individual using sources on the internet. Its name is derived from "Documents" or "Docx". Doxing method is based purely on the ability of the hacker to recognize valuable information about his target and use this information to his benefit. It is also based around the idea that, "The more you know about your target, the easier it will be to find his or her flaws"

Well yeah, he is saying he is doxing me and he talked about one of my youtube channels (he's never talked to me before)

by jtyuprax **December 29, 2011**

(Source: UrbanDictionary.com)

It's simple enough, for example, to run a search for someone, and the work is made even easier if people haven't updated their privacy settings.

Doxing is popular for a variety of reasons, from law enforcement and business analysis to blackmail, harassment, digital shaming and vigilantism. Hacktivist group Anonymous has done much to bring doxing into the public eye. In one instance, they began releasing the identities of members of the Ku Klux Klan.

As with many aspects of social networking, doxing can be a force for both good and evil. It should be noted, though, that doxing isn't illegal. In fact, it relies on gathering information that's already in the public domain, so you could argue that it's not even unethical.

Let's take a quick look at a doxing case study.

Case Study: *Sunil Tripathi Gets Doxed*
Classification: *Privacy*

What Happened:

After the bombing at the Boston Marathon in 2013, Reddit users banded together to try to identify the suspects. One of the suspects that they identified was an American student called Sunil Tripathi who went missing a month before the attack.

Tripathi was eventually found dead in the Providence River, eight days after the bombing. By that point, the perpetrators of the crime had been identified by the FBI as Dzhokhar and Tamerlan Tsarnaev, and Tripathi's name had been cleared. The family later confirmed that Tripathi's death was a result of suicide.

How it Could've Been Avoided:

Doxing is particularly interesting because there's very little that you can do to protect yourself. In Tripathi's case, it's unclear when he died. It's probable that he was already dead by the time that he fell victim to doxing.

The fault here lies largely with the users of Reddit, who implicated Tripathi in the first place. It's something of an ethical grey area, as you could argue both sides. People should have the freedom to make speculations, but they should also have enough common sense to avoid accusing innocent people of murder.

Doxing can sometimes take a more sinister turn. One particularly dangerous trend is "swatting," in which people call the emergency services and claim that a crime is taking place at your address.

This is bad enough in the UK, but it becomes even more dangerous in the US with SWAT teams descending upon suburban houses. These armed response units are typically authorised to shoot to kill, and so as well as wasting valuable resources, swatting can be lethal.

Swatting is particularly common amongst the gaming community. If you're playing a competitive online game such as Call of Duty, it's easy to annoy someone. Plus, a lot of gamers stream live video across the internet, which means that the prankster can actually watch as the police force arrives.

Unfortunately, you're largely at the whim of other people. If they decide to report a crime that didn't happen, it's your word against theirs. In most cases, it's enough to simply hope that it never happens. Most people will never have to worry about swatting in the same way that they're unlikely to be accused of murder.

There are two main reasons why people get swatted. Typically, the victim has argued with someone, or they're successful enough to be on the receiving end of jealousy. Luckily, swatting is highly illegal in most countries. If the perpetrators are caught then they can be charged with a number of different offences, depending upon the circumstances. However, it can be difficult to trace the suspects, so pursuing them is not always practical.

Case Study: *Google Buzz Causes Problems*
Classification: *Privacy*

What Happened:

In 2010, Google launched Google Buzz, a social networking site that was built into Gmail. Buzz, which shut down in 2011 and was eventually replaced by Google+, featured integration with a number of other social networking sites, including Flickr, YouTube, Twitter and FriendFeed. It also allowed you to post updates directly to Buzz.

When users first signed up for Buzz, they were prompted to automatically add all of their e-mail contacts. When they posted from a mobile device, their location was shared so that their contacts could view a map of who was around them.

Unfortunately, these two factors combined to create all sorts of privacy concerns. One particular case centred around a woman whose abusive ex-partner was able to track her down through Google Buzz without her actively giving him permission to read her updates.

How it Could've Been Avoided:

Google has a reputation for not thinking through the practicalities. In this instance, they could have avoided much of the negativity by staggering the launch of Buzz, instead of opening it up to everyone at once. By doing this, they would have been able to gather feedback from real users and to alleviate any privacy fears ahead of the full launch.

Meanwhile, users of the service had the ability to change their privacy settings if they wanted to. It's important to do some research on any new social network before you join it so that you're fully aware of where you stand and what you can do to protect your updates. If Buzz users had researched this before joining the site, many of the issues could have been avoided.

Ultimately, privacy is a hot topic in the new millennium, and it's not just social networking sites that have come under fire. The proliferation of CCTV cameras, particularly in the UK (which has 1% of the world's population and 20% of its CCTV cameras[35]), means that it's literally impossible to live your life off the radar. Especially now that we have to spend so much time online, if not for work then for leisure, pleasure and relationships.

Luckily, most social networking sites make it easy for you to control who can see the information that you post, and there's a lot that you can do if you want to maintain your privacy. Here are just a few of the steps you can take.

---

[35] See: http://www.dailymail.co.uk/news/article-444819/UK-1-worlds-population-20-CCTV-cameras.html

Privacy Settings:

Almost all social networks offer a range of different privacy settings. On Google+, for example, you control which "circles" of friends get to see stuff, and on Facebook you can tighten your settings down so much that it's possible to make things visible only to yourself, so that they can stay private without forcing you to delete them forever. Twitter allows you to have a private profile, as indicated by a padlock symbol. This means that people are unable to follow you or to see your tweets without your explicit approval.

Restraint:

Essentially, you're responsible for your safety. Try to avoid sharing anything that strangers could use against you. This includes your phone number, your address and your e-mail address. Keep those private. If you do need to share them with someone, share them via a private message.

Go Ex-Directory:

Some countries allow you to opt out of directory listings, including both online and offline directories. Consider taking the opportunity, so that it's more difficult for people to track down identifiable information from third-party sources.

Try to Dox Yourself:

Put yourself in the frame of mind of someone who wants to damage your reputation, and try to find as much information as possible through tools such as search engines and social media. If there's something that you're trying to hide, try to research it. If you find content that you're unhappy with, report it to the webmaster or remove it yourself if you're able to.

CHAPTER EIGHT: OTHER PEOPLE

OTHER PEOPLE ARE ASSHOLES. I don't have a study to back this up, but it's a fact. Think about it. Most of the drama and conflict that you experience in your day-to-day life is probably down to the fact that somebody, somewhere, is an asshole.

Unfortunately, on social networking sites, people can be assholes en masse, which is never good. Just look at the comments on the Daily Mail's most shared articles and you'll see exactly what I mean. Other people are assholes. Other people are racist, sexist, xenophobic assholes.

Which makes it something of a surprise that 75.4% of our survey respondents said that they get on with "most people" on social networking sites. We so often hear about arguments and confrontations that it's easy to forget that, in most cases, people are generally quite nice to each other if left to their own devices.

This is backed up by the fact that only 22.4% of people say that they've confronted someone in real life about something that they posted. In general, it's become quite common in our society for us to casually refer to our social networking activity in face to face conversation. "Did you see the video I posted last night?" for example. However, it's less common for people to seek out and to confront someone over something negative, but as our statistics show, it does happen.

In fact, it could easily be argued that the vast majority of our case studies also fit into the category of "other people," because ultimately, social networking boils down to human to human communication. Many of these cases involve people who don't know each other or large groups of people interacting with a single person, such as with a viral video.

In this chapter, we'll be looking specifically at the people that we know, and at examples in which the root cause was human to human interaction between a small group of people. Let's kick things off by looking at a case study.

Case Study: *The Tragic Death of Hannah Smith*
Classification: *Other People*

What Happened:

Ask.fm is a website that allows people to create a profile so that people can ask them questions. As well as allowing people to attach their name to their questions, it also allows them to ask questions anonymously. Because of this, it's attracted some controversy due to young users posting anonymous hate messages in a phenomenon known as cyberbullying.

In one case, a fourteen-year-old British girl was found hanged after being targeted by cyberbullies, who had left comments telling her to "go die," "drink bleach" and "get cancer". There have been similar cases in other countries, including in Italy, where another fourteen-year-old jumped to her death after receiving comments including "kill yourself," "nobody wants you" and "you are not normal."

How it Could've Been Avoided:

There are strong arguments to suggest that Ask.fm should bar anonymous comments from the network, but such policies are hard to implement and, ultimately, just won't solve the problem.

It largely falls down to regulators to enforce stricter penalties for people who are guilty of cyberbullying, and to the social networks, to some extent, to make it easier for people to report and delete offensive comments.

As for the unfortunate user who starts to receive such messages, the best thing to do is to adopt a "do not feed the trolls" mentality. That is, to ignore the messages and to move on with your life. In most cases, responding to people will only fuel the flames and cause the negativity to spiral.

Cyberbullying has been hailed as one of the evils of the internet, and yet that's hardly a fair accusation. After all, there have been bullies for as long as our species cares to remember, and technology is just an enabler, in the same way that a pen and a piece of paper are required if you want to write hate mail.

Unfortunately, due to the widespread adoption of the internet (40% of the world has access to the net at the time of writing[36]), cases of cyberbullying are on the rise, and many governments have been slow to deploy new legislation.

Ultimately, when it comes to cyberbullying, the fault lies with the perpetrators, and without adequate protection in place, it's hard to see how they can be stopped. Sometimes, it's better to simply walk away.

Cyberbullying leads us on to racism, one of the worst aspects of modern society. One campaign by Criola, a civil rights organisation run by Afro-Brazilian women, highlighted the inherent risk of posting racist remarks on social networking sites[37]. They used publicly viewable data to take racist comments and to put them up on billboards, using geolocation technology to make sure that each billboard was near where the post originated. A clever use of technology and enough to make any racist paranoid. Good.

Even when people aren't being assholes, they can still be untrustworthy. In fact, we can't even trust ourselves. Our brains are inherently bad at remembering minor details, and so our recollection of the truth is often biased. This is a problem for the police, as eyewitnesses can contradict each other when recalling variable information, such as the colour of a car or the height of a suspect. People can even be convinced that they committed a crime that never happened[38].

Just over 10% of our survey respondents admitted to lying or exaggerating on social networking sites, a figure which seems low at first glance. But then, if you're willing to lie on social networks, then a survey

---

[36] See: http://www.internetlivestats.com/internet-users/

[37] See: http://www.bbc.co.uk/news/blogs-trending-34945756

[38] See: http://www.psychologicalscience.org/index.php/news/releases/people-can-be-convinced-they-committed-a-crime-they-dont-remember.html

should be easy. Besides we don't always know that we're doing it.

Similarly, just 18.6% of respondents admitted to getting jealous of other people after reading their updates. Now, I'm not ashamed to say that I get jealous. How could you not when friends are on holiday and you're stuck in the office on a dreary Monday morning? But perhaps I'm in the minority.

Option	Responses
I get on with most people on social media	75.44%
I've confronted someone in real life about what they posted	22.42%
I get jealous of what other people post on social media	18.62%
I've lied or exaggerated on social media to impress other people	10.44%

(Source: Survey)

There's another dark side to social networking: catfishing, where someone pretends to be someone else. Catfishes often use fictitious profiles to sell stuff (Ray-Bans, anyone?) or to interact with people that they know in real life under a pseudonym. You might have heard the term before, due to Nev Schulman's successful documentary and television series.

Fortunately, as a user, it's easy to avoid this by only accepting friend requests from people that you actually know and by using a little common sense. And there's a lot you can do to protect yourself. Here are my top tips for staying safe from other people. For maximum effect, use these in combination with the tips from previous sections.

Be Selective:

Simply put, reject friend requests from people that you don't know. At the very least, this will force people to use their real names, which has got to be better than nothing.

Don't Feed the Trolls:

If someone is determined to get into an argument, ignore them. It's not worth the time, stress or effort it takes to deal with them, and doing so usually encourages them to continue

Know Your Rights:

You're probably protected by a number of local and international laws, depending upon where you're based. Laws vary from country to country and change too often to list here, so look them up on a search engine.

CHAPTER NINE: PARANOID BRANDS

SO FAR, we've focused on consumers. We've talked about how to protect ourselves as individuals, and whilst we have looked at brands on occasion, it's largely been to show how they can pose a threat to the average Joe.

But what most people don't realise is that brands are at just as much risk as individuals, and potentially even more so. After all, if a brand collapses then thousands of people could lose their jobs, and it's easily possible for social media to lead to such a scenario. After all, something as simple as a hack, which we've already discussed in chapter three, can cause huge amounts of damage.

In fact, according to a 2015 report by ThreatMetrix, the UK suffers from more cyberattacks than any other country, and there was a 20% increase during 2014. On top of this, human error is involved in more than 95% of security breaches, and 94% of British businesses have been targeted by cyberattacks in the last year.

Take, for example, the Associated Press hack, which we talked about in chapter three. In this example, something as simple as a hacked Twitter account was enough to ensure a 143-point fall in the Dow Jones industrial average.

Case Study: *HMV Employees Live-Tweet Their Dismissals*
Classification: *Image*

What Happened:

After HMV went into administration, the company was forced to downsize. Unfortunately, they also laid off members of the marketing department. Cue a series of disgruntled tweets from HMV's corporate account.

The employees, who were "tweeting live from HR" whilst the team was being fired, posted seven tweets before HMV regained control of the account. One of the tweets read, "There are over 60 of us being fired at once! Mass execution, of loyal employees who love the brand."

How it Could've Been Avoided:

HMV's employees were expected to follow a social networking framework, which explained how to behave online. In fact, this was explicitly referred to in one of the tweets that was posted: "Sorry we've been quiet for so long. Under contract, we've been unable to say a word, or – more importantly – tell the truth."

Unfortunately for HMV, this framework was no longer valid once the employees' contracts were terminated. Executives at the company should have realised this beforehand and taken steps to secure the account, by changing the password and updating the registered e-mail address.

The HMV incident shines a light on one of the most common mistakes that brands make when launching a social presence. Seasoned executives have an irritating habit of assigning social media marketing to the youngest member of the team.

This is exactly what happened at HMV. An intern had been asked to create the account, and no senior staffers were given access. The account grew over time, but the power still lay with a junior member of the team.

And, let's face it, the more junior you are in terms of your position and your experience, the more likely you are to make a mistake. It's also important for your social media team to be familiar with marketing theory. How many interns have heard of user journeys and buying cycles?

Let's take a look at another example of when an inexperienced team member caused a headache for the brand that they worked for.

Case Study: *The American Red Cross Gets Slizzered*
Classification: *Lack of Knowledge*

What Happened:

The American Red Cross took on an intern to manage their social networking profiles, with predictable results. They accidentally tweeted from the Red Cross's profile when they meant to post as themselves. The message?

"Ryan found two more four-bottle packs of Dogfish Head's Midas Touch beer. When we drink we do it right #GettingSlizzered"

Fortunately, the Red Cross was quick to react, and the tweet was soon deleted. They even saw the humour in the situation, posting a tongue-in-cheek response to humanise the brand and to reduce potential damage.

How it Could've Been Avoided:

The incident was partly the Red Cross's fault, as they shouldn't have employed an intern to manage their profiles. However, the intern should have double-checked that they were tweeting from the correct account.

Ultimately, it's likely that this was an accident, but it still highlights the risks that brands face when using social media. Fortunately, the Red Cross had a crisis response plan, so they were able to quickly defuse the situation.

Many brands choose not to bother with social networking at all, but they're wasting an opportunity. Besides, your customers are already discussing your company and comparing it to your competitors. Don't get left out of the conversation!

For brands, social networking sites can be used for customer service, quality assurance, market research, competitor analysis, marketing, and more. The most successful brands have integrated social media across multiple departments, all working in tandem.

Besides, the market is now so saturated that if you're not active on social networking sites then you'll get left behind. And in case you're still not convinced, let's take a look at a company that used social media to great effect.

Case Study: *HubSpot's IPO*
Classification: *N/A*

What Happened:

In 2006, after meeting at MIT, Brian Halligan and Dharmesh Shah formed a company called HubSpot. HubSpot is notable for evangelising inbound marketing, in which companies use helpful, relevant content, such as blog posts, white papers and infographics, to bring in potential customers.

This was a radical departure from outbound marketing, the traditional way of doing things. Outbound marketing relies on interrupting people with advertisements during TV shows, in magazines and on billboards.

Studies have shown that the inbound approach is more effective, with inbound leads costing 61% less than outbound leads[39]. HubSpot

[39] See: http://blog.hubspot.com/blog/tabid/6307/bid/31555/Inbound-Leads-Cost-61-Less-Than-Outbound-New-Data.aspx

eventually went public on the stock exchange at a valuation of $900 million – further proof that inbound marketing can lead to a positive return on investment.

How it Could Be Repeated:

HubSpot has always maintained its stance on the success of inbound marketing, and this authenticity has led to a devoted following which trusts the brand. In fact, HubSpot practices its own techniques to bring in new customers, and it works.

You can also count on HubSpot to have considered all elements of their digital marketing strategy. They've clearly implemented social media policies and hired top talent to manage their profiles.

Social media policies are a necessity for any company that hopes to avoid embarrassment, and simply having one in place is often enough to calm your paranoia. There are all sorts of interesting approaches to writing policies, and it tends to vary by industry.

Companies that work in regulated industries, such as healthcare or finance, will have a much tougher time of things, as they'll face external regulations as well. Still, in my experience, it's easy enough to assimilate any external regulations into your overall policy.

A typical social media policy will list the company's official standpoint on any key issues, and it will explain to employees what they're allowed to say and do on social networking sites. At some companies, employees are required to read and sign such a policy on their first day of work. Whilst it might not sound like it, the goal of these policies is usually to empower employees to use social networking sites and not to stop them from doing so.

Case Study: *Rakesh Agrawal Gets Fired*
Classification: *Lack of Knowledge*

What Happened:

Rakesh Agrawal, PayPal's director of global strategy, posted a series of drunken tweets while at a jazz festival in New Orleans. The tweets were poorly written and verbally abusive towards his colleagues, including Christina Smedley, the company's vice president of global communications.

Agrawal later attempted to mitigate his behaviour with a number of excuses, including sleep deprivation, work stress and long hours, as well as the design of Twitter and the layout of his new phone.

How it Could've Been Avoided:

Agrawal could have avoided the situation by following the Grandma Rule or by not using social sites whilst intoxicated. PayPal came out of this with their reputation intact, but only because they had the correct policies in place.

The company swiftly dismissed the employee, issuing a statement to say, "Rakesh Agrawal is no longer with the company. Treat everyone with respect. No excuses. PayPal has zero tolerance."

Many companies also implement a crisis response policy. These policies outline the approach that a company will take when responding to an incident, whether it's a real world crisis, such as the death of a customer, or a social networking crisis, such as Agrawal's Twitter rant.

Fortunately, as we've already seen, it's not impossible for brands to recover from a disaster or at least to mitigate some of the damage. We'll continue to take a look at how brands have managed to do this in the coming chapters where we'll explore how social paranoia affects organisations and how some real-world brands have managed to deal with it.

CHAPTER TEN: SCAREMONGERING

TO SOME EXTENT we're about to get meta, because this chapter deals with the portrayals of corporate social networking that we're used to seeing in the media. The vast majority of brands use social networking sites without incident, but because that's not necessarily newsworthy, we don't often hear about it.

Nevertheless, marketers in particular are often exposed to horror stories about what happens when social networking goes wrong, on websites like TechCrunch and Mashable and in books like this one. In fact, 63.1% of our survey respondents have heard stories about brands making mistakes on social, and it seems likely that the figure will continue to increase over time.

Let's face it. Nobody's perfect, and a company is a collection of imperfect people who are working towards a common goal. Mistakes will inevitably be made. Social networking is now a part of our day-to-day lives, and so mistakes have become routine. People still write about them, though.

Unfortunately for brands, mistakes on social networking sites can have real world consequences in terms of lost customers and lost revenue. Twenty-seven percent of our survey respondents have stopped buying from a brand after something that they posted, which is a sizeable percentage.

But as we've already discussed, social networking sites have their positive sides, too. If you avoid using them because you're afraid of losing revenue, you'll lose revenue anyway because of the missed opportunity.

One of the interesting things about scaremongering is that it usually centres on large, international businesses. Don't be lulled into a false sense of security. Small businesses can be vulnerable too, as is the case with Amy's Baking Company Bakery Boutique & Bistro from Scottsdale, Arizona. Amy's is notorious for having one of the most epic brand meltdowns of all time, and we'll be taking a closer look at this in chapter fifteen when we take a look at public image.

scaremonger
/ˈskɛːmʌŋgə/

noun

a person who spreads frightening or ominous reports or rumours.
"scaremongers forecast that 8 m–9 m people could soon flood in"
synonyms: **alarmist**, prophet of doom, Cassandra, voice of doom, **doom-monger**;
More

(Source: Google.com)

According to one report by EU Kids Online, a team of academics from the London School of Economics, the media's focus on the more extreme aspects of social networking is distracting people from digital education. Education is important to help young people to become digital natives and to learn transferable, technology-based skills.

"The media is the main source of the information apart from safety lessons in schools," explains Leslie Haddon, one of the report's authors[40]. "One of the things that often comes up is 'stranger danger.'"

Interestingly, this mirrors how many brands feel. They've heard the horror stories, and the subsequent paranoia can lead to people shying away from marketing, just in case. This is an observable phenomenon, too. One study by the Internet Advertising Bureau found that 33% of marketers avoid programmatic, one of the latest trends in digital marketing, because of brand safety limitations[41].

---

[40] See: http://www.wired.co.uk/news/archive/2014-06/05/eu-kids-online-safety-report-media-scaremongering

[41] See: http://digitalmarketingmagazine.co.uk/digital-marketing-advertising/don-t-damage-your-brand-know-your-limitations-online

Case Study: *Vodafone's Andrew Morfill Speaks Out*
Classification: *Scaremongering*

What Happened:

Andrew Morfill is Vodafone's Cyber Threat Intelligence Manager, and his job is to deal with social paranoia by making the company's systems as secure as possible. Morfill, who was in the Army before joining Vodafone's global risk team, explains: "Vodafone is the 13th biggest brand in the world and operates in 26 countries. We do not want to be in the papers for data breaches, nor do we want the heavy fines that can come with that."[42]

This echoes the hacks and leaks that we looked at in earlier chapters. Andrew's job is to reduce the risk of such attacks, and to pick up on them quickly if they do happen. He says, "It can be 260-290 days before a company realises it's lost valuable information, and the implications of that can be huge."

How it Could've Been Avoided:

In a company the size of Vodafone, there's a real need for such a role because there's so much that could go wrong. This isn't a case of paranoia. After all, telecommunications brands are second only to financial institutions in terms of how much abuse they receive, at least anecdotally. It's a smart move on Vodafone's part to establish such a position.

---

[42] See: https://www.officersassociation.org.uk/blogs/cyber-security-isnt-just-scaremongering/

For smaller companies, the need to hire someone in a cybersecurity position is counteracted by the reduced risk of attack and the fact that many third-party data centres will take care of security for you. However, you may still be liable for any damages, and so even if you don't have a dedicated employee who's in charge of cybersecurity, you still need someone who's responsible for creating any policies and protocols that you might need to deal with an attack, should it happen.

Because of the risks involved, to consumers and to brands, you could argue that companies just don't belong on social networks. In fact, 15.5% of our survey respondents believe that brands should stay away from social.

We've already discussed some of the benefits for brands when it comes to social networking, but we haven't looked at things from a consumer's perspective. After all, if your favourite brands are active on social networking sites, it can be hugely beneficial. You might find it easier to get help if you have a problem, or you might be offered discount vouchers for future purchases.

People see branded social networking as a double-edged sword. It can be useful, but it can also be annoying. It falls to the brand to ensure that they're as useful as possible. This includes giving your followers the ability to easily opt out of messaging and to provide them with the most relevant content that you can.

Option	Responses
I've heard stories about brands making mistakes on social	63.09%
I've stopped buying from a brand after something they've posted	27.00%
Brands don't belong on social	15.47%
I follow my employer on social	16.69%

(Source: Survey)

A similar, surprisingly low percentage of respondents (16.7%) said that they follow their employer on social networking sites. The reason for this figure is unclear. Perhaps it's because people don't want to be reminded of work in their leisure time or perhaps their jobs just aren't that important to them.

It seems forgivable for people who work at McDonald's, for example, to avoid following their employer's Facebook page. After all, if you have a minimum wage job at a global organisation, then it's unlikely you're particularly passionate. If you're a marketing manager, though, then you need to know what's being said, when it's being said, and who it's being said to.

Another potential explanation is the fact that some employers aren't on social in the first place. Part of this could be down to self-employment, which is on the rise at the time of writing with almost half of new job roles being self-employed[43]. When you're running your own business, marketing often takes on a low priority because there are so many other things to worry about. As a consequence, many self-employed workers go without.

This brings me to another interesting subject – the negativity bias. The negativity bias (or the negativity effect) is a concept that was first proposed by Paul Rozin and Edward Royzman[44]. Loosely speaking, it refers to the way that things of a more negative nature, such as unpleasant thoughts and negative emotions, have a greater effect on your state of mind than things that are neutral or positive.

Because of this, something positive tends to have less of an impact on your life than something negative that's of an equal intensity. It's also been observed that a combination of negative and positive events tends to lead to a skewed interpretation that places greater emphasis on the negativity. In other words, the whole is more negative than the sum of its parts.

The negativity bias is an observable phenomenon, and so simply knowing about it might be enough to combat it. It's easy to see how this same bias could affect business decisions – how often is a great idea

---

[43] See: http://www.newstatesman.com/politics/2015/01/being-self-employed-becoming-new-normal.

[44] See: http://psr.sagepub.com/content/5/4/296.refs

scuppered, for example, because an executive could only see potential problems?

This negativity bias, when combined with the effects of social paranoia, hints at exactly why some marketers have such a hard time getting approval for their campaigns. Arguably, senior employees also have much more to lose, at least in terms of their salary. Because of this, it can often seem easier to remain inactive than to risk something going wrong. But while that might work well in the short term, it'll give your competitors a huge advantage over the coming years as social networking becomes more and more important.

Still, there's no need to panic. As we've seen throughout the book, there's plenty you can do to protect yourself. While scaremongering is unlikely to go away, you shouldn't let it put you off. Here are a few steps that you can take to stay safe.

Learn from others' mistakes...

Just because the media pounces on the tiniest of mistakes, it doesn't mean that you shouldn't read what they say about it. In fact, you can learn from the mistakes that other people have made and then use that knowledge to stop the same thing from happening to you.

...but don't let the coverage get to you:

Take everything that you read with a pinch of salt. It's not all true, and even when it is true, it's usually a worst-case scenario. It's the same as when you read stories about terror attacks in a newspaper. You shouldn't allow it to affect you to the point that you're too terrified to leave your house.

Take time for a reality check:

If you're a smaller brand, or one that works in a relatively boring industry, it's unlikely that you'll cause enough of a furore to hit the national news. If you're worried about the scaremongering that you see around you, take a second to ask yourself whether anyone would have noticed if you'd made the same mistake.

Have processes in place to cover yourself:

We've talked about processes and policies in previous chapters. These should say what you can and can't say, so that if something does go wrong you can identify who was at fault. You can use the written policies as backup if you need to escalate the incident to a disciplinary level.

Take the time to speak to decision-makers:

Carve out some time to speak to the people who are in charge of your department, and ensure that they know that scaremongering is just that. Identify any possible areas of concern and find solutions to those problems so that they're fully supportive of your social media marketing efforts.

CHAPTER ELEVEN: LACK OF KNOWLEDGE

A LACK OF KNOWLEDGE is the reason for a large amount of social paranoia, and the purpose of this book is to educate its readers to combat it. Ultimately, social networking sites evolve so rapidly that it's virtually impossible for us, as users and as marketers, to keep up with them.

One of the main areas where a lack of knowledge can have a real world impact is when it comes to spelling mistakes and typos. In fact, 58% of our survey respondents get annoyed by typos. In 2011, it was reported that poor spelling costs UK businesses millions of pounds in lost revenue[45].

As an aside, I'm one of the people who's put off by typos. I suppose it comes with the territory when you're a writer. If I see a typo on a retailer's website, it suggests that they're untrustworthy – and that the business doesn't care enough to proofread – and I'm hesitant to give them my payment details. I'd rather find the same product somewhere else, so that I can buy from someone who can spell. As my editor, Pam Harris, says, "This is why people need editors. Typos are evil and must be destroyed." But then, she would say that.

When brands can't spell, it also hints that there might be a junior employee behind the wheel, which we've already talked about. It's not exactly ideal. When asked, only 28.2% of survey respondents agreed that brands know what they're doing on social media, which reflects the general sense of consumer unease that brands are still battling against.

But it's not just typos that brands have to worry about .A lack of knowledge when it comes to account security and password protection can lead to hacks and leaks, for example, which can affect companies and

---

[45] See: http://www.bbc.co.uk/news/education-14130854

consumers alike. In the case study that we're about to look at, a lack of knowledge means that we still don't understand what happened.

Case Study: *Roger Ebert Comes Back from the Dead*
Classification: *Lack of Knowledge*

What Happened:

When film critic Roger Ebert passed away in 2013, control of his Twitter account passed over to his wife. The account remained mostly dormant, posting occasional promotional material, until August of 2015, when the account posted a series of mysterious tweets[46], including one which read: "This account is eating up all of my data. Please respond."

Even more bizarrely, contextual responses were also posted from the account, suggesting that Chaz Ebert, Roger Ebert's wife, was the one who was in control, although it's never been confirmed or denied. The tweets were still online at the time of writing.

How it Could've Been Avoided:

It seems likely that the posts came from Chaz Ebert and that she thought she was logged into her own account. This is yet another reason to check which account you're posting from before you hit the tweet button.

For brands, a lack of knowledge can also tie in with something that we'll look at in a later chapter – a lack of ROI (return on investment). Poorly educated marketers have a tendency to jump into social networking without

---

[46] See: http://thenextweb.com/shareables/2015/08/10/i-do-not-fear-death-most-of-the-time/

any forethought in a way that you don't see anywhere else. Nobody runs a TV ad on a whim, for example. If you don't know why you're using social networking, there's no way to measure your success, so how will you know whether you're wasting your money?

But the biggest brand fails are the humongous mistakes that we see in the media on a day-to-day basis and form the foundation of the scaremongering that we see, which we've already discussed. From time to time, brands make such monumental cock-ups that it's hard to tell how they managed it, other than through sheer ignorance. Let's take a look at one of those now.

Case Study: *Celeb Boutique Tries to Piggyback a Trend*
Classification: *Lack of Knowledge*

What Happened:

In July 2012, Celeb Boutique attempted to join in on a trending topic by using the #Aurora hashtag. Unfortunately, #Aurora was trending because a gunman entered a screening of *The Dark Knight Rises* in Aurora, Colorado, and opened fire on the audience. Celeb Boutique's tweet read: "#Aurora is trending, clearly about our Kim K inspired #Aurora dress ;)"

The company deleted the tweet, but the damage had already been done. They responded to the criticism with a series of tweets which read: "We're incredibly sorry for our tweet about Aurora. Our PR is NOT US-based and had not checked the reason for the trend. At the time our social media was totally UNAWARE of the situation and simply thought it was another trending topic. We have removed the very insensitive tweet and will, of course, take more care in the future to look into what we say in our tweets. Again, we do apologise for any offence caused, this was not intentional and will not occur again. Our most sincere apologies for both the tweet and situation."[47]

How it Could've Been Avoided:

Whilst Celeb Boutique's response was measured and well-executed, they could have avoided the problem to begin with by spending thirty seconds browsing through tweets that other users had posted using the hashtag. Their failure to do this caused a large amount of damage to the brand, and it ultimately left a lasting bad memory in the minds of consumers.

A poor social networking presence can have real world impacts when it comes to revenue. If you make a high-profile mistake then people might boycott your brand, reducing both existing and potential revenue.

In fact, 40% of survey respondents said that a bad social networking presence is enough to put them off a purchase. Think about it. How quickly would you react if your packaging was alienating 40% of your customers? And why should social networking be any different?

Admittedly, our respondents also appreciate the difficulties that brands can face with only 27.3% of them believing that they could run a branded Facebook page. This suggests that the majority of people understand the effort that needs to go into a sophisticated social networking presence, and it's likely that this is due, in part, to the number of mistakes that they hear about.

Option	Responses
I think brands know what they're doing on social	28.24%
I get annoyed by typos	58.07%

[47] See: http://www.huffingtonpost.com/2012/07/20/celebboutique-tweet-colorado-batman-shooting_n_1690308.html

A bad social presence puts me off buying	39.98%
I think I could run a brand's Facebook page	27.26%

(Source: Survey)

One of the biggest problems for both brands and consumers is the risk of mistakes that have real world consequences. We hear about this every now and then, when brands fail to take care of their customers' data because somebody, somewhere, made a mistake.

Arguably, the case of Bradley Manning, the American soldier who released huge amounts of data to WikiLeaks and hit headlines across the world, was brought about by a lack of knowledge. American governmental policy changed after September 11th in an effort to enable the sharing of data between different departments to stop a similar tragedy from happening.

However, this approach led to their undoing because it meant that Manning was able to access all sorts of files that he didn't need to. Worse, it wasn't exactly a secret. Trading files was almost commonplace, and whilst Manning did need to use sophisticated methods to cover his tracks, it would have been possible for tens of thousands of servicemen to leak the data that he eventually released.

Case Study: *Tesco Hits the Hay*
Classification: *Lack of Knowledge*

What Happened:

In January of 2013, Tesco was already suffering from a PR disaster after it emerged that some of their burgers contained horsemeat. Their social media team was facing abuse and ridicule, and the battered brand was struggling to deal with the fallout from the scandal.

Then, they posted a tweet which appeared to make light of the issue, which read: "It's sleepy time so we're off to hit the hay! See you at 8am for more #TescoTweets". Cue all sorts of outraged responses from the general public.

How it Could've Been Avoided:

The damaging post was scheduled way before the scandal, but in their rush to deal with the sudden onslaught of negativity, Tesco's employees forgot to cancel it. During any crisis, you should cancel all preset activity as a priority. Better still, don't preset posts in the first place!

As we've discussed in this chapter, there are plenty of reasons to be paranoid about a lack of knowledge when it comes to social networking. After all, there's always something to learn, and there's no realistic way to ensure full education for your employees. That said, there are a few steps that you can take to stay abreast of the latest developments and best practices.

Follow the social networking sites that you use:

Follow each of the social networking sites that you use, and be sure to check out their blogs and their help centres. Most sites provide all the information you need because it's in their best interests to keep users safe. If you're not impressed by their help centres, then don't use their service.

Read blogs:

There are plenty of fantastic blog sites that are dedicated to the latest in social networking news. Google it and see what you can find, or check out some of my favourites: Mashable, TechCrunch, ReadWriteWeb, TheNextWeb, SearchEngineLand and Wired.

Don't believe everything you read:

It's easy to post things on the internet, and people don't always check the accuracy of information before they share it. Just because you read something, it doesn't make it true, so have a look around and try to verify the information before you take it seriously.

If in doubt, get out:

If something doesn't feel right, trust your gut instincts and get out of there. It's better to be safe than sorry, and this is especially important for brands, when a simple mistake can cost millions of pounds in lost revenue.

Plan for failure, just in case:

We've talked about this elsewhere in the book. Establish a crisis response protocol, just in case something goes wrong. If you know how you're going to react in an emergency then you can leap into action if something goes wrong.

CHAPTER TWELVE: RISK VS REWARD

RISK VS REWARD. This is a hot topic amongst marketers because when you're doing something for a living, you need to do it properly. There are some marketers who are doing exciting things with virtual reality and personalisation, but there are others who have neither the budget nor the authority to commit to such ambitious projects.

We've already learned about a lot of the problems that social media marketers have to face, and we still have plenty of pages to go, so you should be well aware of the risks by now. But we haven't focused on the advantages. After all, this book is primarily about the risk, rather than the reward.

Let's take a quick look at a brand that stumbled into social media and managed to turn a negative into a positive. Let's take a quick look at Dell.

Case Study: *Dell Hell and Heaven*
Classification: *Risk vs Reward*

What Happened:

In June 2005, Jeff Jarvis wrote a blog post about his experience with Dell. Jarvis, who was already an influential blogger, ranted at length about the poor customer service that the company offered, saying: "Dell sucks. Dell lies. Put that in your Google and smoke it."

Since then, Dell has improved its approach to public relations and social media. It's also received acclaim for Ideastorm, a platform which allows people to make suggestions on improvements and to vote on their favourite submissions.

As of March 2012, Ideastorm had received almost fifteen thousand suggestions and led to five hundred refinements at the company[48].

How it Could've Been Avoided:

These days, many brands treat everyone as an influencer. Simply put, it's so hard to tell what might go viral that it's best to treat every customer as though they have the power to cause a major incident. In this case, Dell could have defused the situation by responding promptly and offering to correct the problem that Jarvis was complaining about. Unfortunately, they didn't.

But at least they learned from the experience, and Ideastorm is a great example of a company encouraging involvement from its users. Better still, Dell acted on the feedback. Many of the tweaks were minor, but some of them, such as ensuring that members of its global support team are fluent in the language that callers speak, have obvious benefits.

Almost three quarters of our survey respondents (73.8%) said that they understand why brands use social networking sites, and so it seems clear that the majority of people see their value. The debate around measurability has largely been resolved by digital marketers because sales can now be tied back to their source, whether it's a post on a social network or a banner ad on a website. That said, public opinion seems to be divided with just over half (52.1%) of people agreeing that social networking is a good way to sell things.

Sales is usually the ultimate goal for social media marketers, and so it's worrying that only half of people agree that the reward is worth the risk. That said, in business, everything is a risk.

As a professional marketer, one of the things that interests me is the fact

---

[48] See: http://www.forbes.com/sites/shelisrael/2012/03/27/dell-modernizes-ideastorm/

that social media usage can lead to a positive return on investment (ROI) without selling any product. For example, if you're a software company, you could empower your customers to answer each other's questions, saving time and resources for your customer service team. We'll take a look at a case study about that in a minute.

There's also the risk of inactivity to consider. By remaining static and being too scared to move, you can put yourself in danger. Just look at what happened when Napster came out and allowed people to share and discover music in a new (albeit often illegal) way. Instead of embracing the technology and trying to make it profitable for artists and record labels, the music industry tried to shut it down. Then, iTunes and Spotify came out and reinvented the industry on the record labels' behalf, leaving many of the established players behind.

Ultimately, when it comes to business, everything is a risk. You might as well try to get a reward whilst you're at it.

Case Study: *InfusionSoft*
Classification: *Risk vs Reward*

What Happened:

InfusionSoft was able to use social networking to reduce the cost of customer service. They used to need one employee for every 72 customers, but they were able to reduce that to one per 172 customers through the use of social technologies.

As if that wasn't enough, their customer satisfaction rating increased by 10%, which is an impressive feat. They managed to improve satisfaction despite reducing the size of their team. Through doing this, they were able to make substantial savings in terms of salary costs.

How it Could Be Repeated:

The first step is to start to carry out more customer service on social media sites and to see where that leads you. That said, there are a few precautions to take in a situation like this if you want to avoid problems later on.

For example, it's important to make sure that reducing the size of the customer service team has no ill effect on customer satisfaction or the performance of your company. Monitor your results and act accordingly.

It's not just the risk of making a mistake that brands have to worry about. Sometimes consumers are out to get you, too. A surprisingly large proportion of survey respondents – 17.2% – claimed that they'd reported or complained about a brand on a social networking site. Meanwhile, 36.2% of people said that they've bought from a brand that they follow.

Option	Responses
I understand why brands use social media	73.78%
Social media is a good way to sell stuff	52.08%
I've reported or complained about a brand I follow	17.20%
I've bought from a brand I follow	35.23%

(Source: Survey)

It's important to stress that social media marketing isn't for everyone and that it pays to use a little common sense. That said, there's a strong case to be made for at least 90% of organisations. Business-to-business (B2B) brands, which earn their money from making sales to other companies, typically find social media marketing more difficult, but it's not impossible.

As an aside here, most B2B companies are weaker than business-to-consumer (B2C) companies at social media marketing but better than them at content marketing and lead generation. The industry best-practice is for companies to capture the names and contact details of potential buyers by providing useful, relevant content, such as a white paper or a webinar, in exchange for data from the customer, such as their e-mail address or telephone number.

Let's take a look at a case study about a brand that reaped the rewards of social media marketing.

+

Case Study: *Social Media Saves Cisco $100,000*
Classification: *Risk vs Reward*

What Happened:

Cisco managed to save themselves over $100,000 on a product launch by using social media and digital marketing, including virtual reality on Second Life, where they staged a prelaunch concert featuring seven bands over eight hours[49]. This was in sharp contrast to their usual method, which relied heavily on costly placements in newspapers and magazines.

The launch saved Cisco a vast amount of money, but it also helped them to reach more people. Effectively, the campaign cost less money and produced greater results than traditional methods.

How it Could Be Repeated:

As with other case studies in this section, this isn't something that you'd want to avoid. For Cisco, launching a product through social media might have seemed like a risk at first, but with a lower initial investment, they trod carefully and measured their results. One factor to consider here is the response from the general public. It's almost impossible to tell how people might react to a campaign, and so any brand should be prepared to deal with negativity, just in case. With a bit of luck, it won't be a problem!

As usual, we'll end this chapter with a few tips to help you to stay safe

---

[49] See: http://www.socialmediaexaminer.com/cisco-social-media-product-launch/

when it comes to risk vs reward. Remember, the goal here is to minimise the risk and to maximise the potential reward.

Know the risk:

You've made a good start by picking up a copy of *Social Paranoia*, but the hard work doesn't stop there. Spend some time getting to grips with any potential complications, and decide how to deal with them ahead of time. Knowing as much as you can about potential pitfalls will help you to dodge them before they happen and to react quickly if they're unavoidable.

Know the reward:

Likewise, you need to know what you're aiming for. Do you want to sell products or to offer customer service? Whatever your goal is, you need to know how to measure it so that you can determine whether you've achieved it.

Benchmark:

Benchmarking refers to analysing your performance at its base level before you run any campaigns. If you log the performance of your key performance indicators (KPIs) at the beginning, it becomes much easier to spot any changes along the way.

Monitor and audit progress:

Information is useless unless you act upon it. Be sure to keep track of your performance over time and to use any changes to make informed decisions about the future. Keep track of progress and make sure that all marketing activity brings you closer to your goal.

CHAPTER THIRTEEN: COST VS ROI

IN MANY WAYS, this chapter is an evolution of the last one. After all, any investment is a risk, and a return on investment is a reward. But cost vs ROI deserves a chapter of its own because it's a vital topic for marketers and because there's such a wealth of information on the subject.

First, though, let's define the two terms. When we talk about cost, at least in this chapter, we're referring to several different types of cost – the investment cost, the potential cost of any damage to a company's reputation, and the potential cost to shareholders if a scandal occurs. There are many different types of cost, and they don't always involve money.

ROI, or return on investment, is the term for a formula that marketers use to determine whether a campaign was successful. In layman's terms, if the return that you get (in terms of sales or other financial gains) is larger than the cost of a campaign, then the campaign has been a success.

Our survey respondents were divided when it came to recognising the value of a social networking presence with 51.5% of them agreeing that social media is a good investment. In addition, 59.6% of them said that if they launched their own company, they'd use social media marketing.

This divide isn't surprising, as social networking is still relatively new to us and people are still struggling to understand how the technologies can help them to promote their businesses. Besides, our survey respondents aren't all marketers. For marketers, social networking is a hot topic, but consumers tend to use the services without putting too much thought into it.

Still, it's encouraging to note that almost 60% of people would use social networking for their own business if they were to launch one. It's a clear sign of the importance of social networking for marketing. In fact, 40 million small businesses have presences on Facebook alone, according to a 2015 study[50].

Case Study: *Old Spice Sets the Bar High*
Classification: *Risk vs Reward*

What Happened:

Old Spice gained notoriety through their social media campaigns, one of which involved sending personalised video messages to their followers by answering questions and responding to their tweets with videos. The campaign led to a 27% increase on sales, as well as a spike in the final month of the campaign.

The campaign was such a success that Old Spice set a precedent for future campaigns, and a number of other brands have since embraced the concept of personalised video messaging, including KLM.

How it Could Be Repeated:

This is a rare case study where there was almost no risk to the brand. The success of the campaign can be attributed to the fact that Old Spice was the first company to successfully deploy personalised video on a large scale.

The main risk to Old Spice was cost, but when you think about the amount of money that they used to invest in TV ads, it's easy to see how a personalised video campaign could seem attractive.

Consumers are well aware of the costs of social media marketing. In fact, only 18.97% of our survey respondents think that it costs brands nothing. In

---

[50] See: http://marketingland.com/facebook-now-has-40m-active-small-business-pages-126949

fact, in the Old Spice example that we just talked about, despite the relatively low cost when compared to traditional advertisements, the approach would still be out of the question for most small businesses.

That's why many smaller businesses opt to use guerilla marketing, which relies on a low budget approach that doesn't necessarily follow the typical rules of marketing. After all, it's free to sign up to a social networking site and to start posting. It's just that you'll also need to consider the time and resources that it takes to create content, as well as the potential cost of advertisements.

Social media marketing isn't free, then, but it can be used as a low budget tool to communicate a message, and it's often the smaller companies that create the most effective campaigns.

Option	Responses
Social media is a good investment	51.48%
My company has made a profit from social media	12.26%
I think marketing on social media costs brands nothing	18.97%
If I launched my own company, I'd use social media marketing	59.61%

(Source: Survey)

Social networking is a key element of inbound marketing, a form of marketing that relies on bringing customers to your business through the creation of high quality content. For example, someone might discover you because their friend shared one of your posts or they might find your blog through a Google search.

This contrasts with outbound marketing, which is what most people are more familiar with. Outbound marketing relies on interrupting consumers by pushing your message in front of them. Examples of this include television and radio advertisements, print ads and even banner ads.

When it comes to cost vs ROI, inbound marketing is far more efficient for the vast majority of companies, as is revealed by multiple reports from HubSpot. HubSpot, as you'll remember from chapter nine, pioneered the inbound marketing approach, and they've used it to grow a huge business in less than ten years.

Case Study: Cars.com Uses Ratings and Reviews
Classification: Cost vs ROI

What Happened:

A lot of brands are unsure whether to allow reviews on their websites. After all, this could open the brand up to negativity. However, a number of studies have shown that consumers trust reviewers and that they're more likely to trust the reviews if there are occasional negatives.

Cars.com found that adding ratings and reviews for the vehicles in their inventory led to twice as many visitors and an increase of 16% in the number of sales. Whilst it took time and resources to add the review system, it's easy to see how it would eventually pay for itself.

How it Could Be Repeated:

Adding reviews to your website can cost a large amount of money, so you'll want to weigh up the cost vs the potential ROI. Then there's the problem of policing them. It's a good idea to hold reviews for moderation before publishing them, to implement a profanity filter, and to allow users to flag reviews as inappropriate. If people are willing to read and post reviews, then it's likely that they'll also be happy to help you to monitor their quality.

So, how can you protect yourself as a brand when it comes to cost vs ROI? Let's take a look at a few top tips to get you started.

Log your spending:

To get a truly accurate idea of your ROI, you need to keep a proper log of all of the money that you spend. This includes agency costs, advertisements, the cost of prizes and even the cost of stock images. Log everything in one central database so that the information is available to all members of the marketing team.

Monitor your campaigns in real-time:

Use analytical data to make sure that you always know how much money you've generated through sales. Then, combine this with your spending log to determine your return on investment. Monitor this over time, preferably by logging the statistics on a daily basis.

If you commit, commit:

There's nothing worse than a marketing campaign that fails because the company lost its nerve. If you're going to do something, you need to do it properly. If you're cutting elements of the campaign before it launches, you're setting yourself up for failure. The more cohesive and comprehensive your plan is, the more likely it is to work. Cutting elements for budgetary reasons often makes it harder for you to generate a positive ROI.

Remember Seth Godin's Dip:

Successful marketing speaker and author Seth Godin has released a book called *The Dip*, which explains when you should stick and when you should quit. Essentially, you need to monitor the performance of your campaign and to determine a point at which you'd call it off. Then stick to it. Otherwise, you might find yourself endlessly investing time and money into a campaign that will never deliver the ROI that you're looking for.

CHAPTER FOURTEEN: REGULATIONS

REGULATIONS ARE SCARY THINGS. In fact, for organisations within certain sectors like healthcare and finance, they can bring your social media marketing efforts to a halt before they even begin, although there are usually ways to work around them.

I once worked for a skincare brand that was using social networking to support its acne creams. We were up against all sorts of regulations, and we had to report any unexpected side effects. If someone said it gave their skin a healthy glow, we'd have to report it because that's not what the product was supposed to do. It was supposed to combat spots and acne, and nothing else.

We were also unable to sell the product through social media. We could offer support, but we couldn't tell people to buy it. Fortunately, many people bought the product after a recommendation from a pharmacist, and so we created a separate campaign to provide information to pharmacists and to general practitioners, as well as to consumers themselves.

And it's not just pharmaceutical companies that face regulation. Developments like the right to be forgotten ruling in Europe, which we discussed back in chapter six, are having a serious impact on the way that all sorts of organisations are able to operate. In fact, over half (50.1%) of respondents say that they're worried about the internet being regulated by governments.

Interestingly, a surprisingly high percentage (31.2%) of people reported working in a regulated industry, whilst a similar percentage (34%) of respondents said that they're aware of a corporate social media policy for their company. However, whilst these two figures are at similar levels, they don't necessarily correlate. Not everybody who works in a regulated industry is aware of a corporate social media policy, and not everyone who is aware of a corporate social media policy is working in a regulated industry.

In the end, policy creation often falls to the companies themselves. Whilst it's a good idea to have a policy in place, they're usually only needed to cover the company and its employees in case something goes wrong. One thing to bear in mind, though, is that this is another form of regulation, and that there can be plenty of that to begin with.

Option	Responses
I'm worried about freedom on the internet being regulated by governments	50.14%
I work in a regulated industry (i.e. finance, healthcare)	31.21%
My company has a social media policy (that I'm aware of)	34.04%
I know my employer's stance on social media updates	29.66%

(Source: Survey)

In recent years, perhaps the most important regulatory development has been the defeat of SOPA and PIPA. SOPA (the Stop Online Piracy Act) and PIPA (the Prevention of Internet Piracy Act) were two bills put forward by the American government to try to prevent piracy and cybercrime.

Unfortunately, the bills were heavy-handed, and they threatened to derail the very foundations of some of the world's most useful websites. A number of high profile organisations, including Reddit and Google, took part in an organised protest against the bills, and Wikipedia took the step of blocking access to its articles as an example of what might happen if the bills were passed.

At first, it seemed as though the bills would be impossible to stop, but citizens of the internet banded together to inundate congress with complaints and SOPA and PIPA were eventually defeated in a historic example of the power of the people.

Let's look at a quick case study on how regulations can affect social media marketers.

Case Study: *The OFT Clamps Down*
Classification: *Regulations*

What Happened:

In January of 2011, the Office of Fair Trading (OFT) began to crack down on Twitter users (primarily celebrities and bloggers) who were using their profiles to promote products and services without disclosing that they were being paid to do so[51].

This isn't the only case of such a crackdown. In fact, authorities in multiple countries have taken action against people for failing to disclose relationships, and Amazon has even been known to remove book reviews if the reviewer failed to state that they knew the author.

How it Could've Been Avoided:

If you're a blogger or if you're teaming up with one, it's best to ensure that any partnerships are fully disclosed. There's nothing wrong with posting an honest review, but it's in the best interests of both parties to ensure that they comply with regulations by disclosing whether a fee was paid or a product was provided.

One of the big problems with regulations, particularly for companies, is that if you fail to comply with them, you can face legal action and large fines. You have a responsibility, as a marketer, to ensure that you're well aware of all regulations that affect you because ignorance is no excuse in a court of

---

[51] See: http://www.theguardian.com/technology/2011/jan/09/oft-clampdown-covert-twitter-endorsements

law.

Unfortunately, the explosive growth of social networking has outpaced the development of many legal systems, and so there are plenty of archaic laws in Britain, the USA and elsewhere in the world that no longer make sense when they're applied to social networking.

This is an ever-evolving situation, and the only way to keep abreast of it is to spend time reading up on the latest trends, even if you only do it once a week whilst drinking a cup of coffee.

Case Study: *Sony Gets Fined Over Data Protection Act Breach*
Classification: *Regulations*

What Happened:

Sony was fined £250,000 after the Information Commissioners Office found them guilty of allowing a serious breach of the Data Protection Act to occur on the PlayStation Network. The breach allowed hackers to obtain and expose a large amount of personal data, including names, addresses, dates of birth and credit card information.

Of course, this breach was hardly intentional, and the fine that Sony was given was almost certainly easier to swallow than the damage to their reputation, as well as the potential lost revenue from customers who no longer trust the PlayStation Network.

How it Could've Been Avoided:

The best way to prevent attacks such as these is to work with a specialised agency to ensure that you're fully compliant. This is only worth considering if you're a large company with your own payment gateway, such as Apple with iTunes and Google with Google Play.

For most marketers, using common sense and checking local laws should be enough. Agencies, for example, have no problem familiarising themselves with different industries to ensure compliance for clients. It can be learned, but it takes time.

Regulations and local laws are beyond the scope of this book because they change too quickly and would take up too much space. For us, it's enough to know that regulatory compliance can keep marketers awake at night, and that it's one of many contributing factors towards social paranoia.

Case Study: *Facebook Ordered to Stop Collecting Information On Non-Users*
Classification: *Regulations*

What Happened:

Facebook is no stranger to arguments about how they handle their data. In one set of legal cases that targeted Facebook and several other companies, they were criticised for gathering data on people who weren't users of the service but who visited a page on the network.

Facebook does this to improve the advertisements that it serves by making them more relevant for its visitors. However, it was argued that this was in breach of data protection laws, and a court in Brussels ordered the company to stop collecting digital information about non-users. The company was also subjected to a fine of $270,000 per day if it failed to comply[52].

How it Could've Been Avoided:

This one is difficult to call, as it's a landmark case that covers a legal grey area. In many ways, the conflict was inevitable. Facebook is unlikely to bow down to such a ruling because that could seriously affect the company's

[52] See: http://www.lexology.com/library/detail.aspx?g=05bc5cd9-c4f2-4acf-8c4c-54fb7db3d7f6

future. As a society, we're still not sure how to deal with concerns about privacy. Only time will tell how we come to some sort of compromise.

So how do you protect yourself in a world that's full of regulations? Here are a few tips to get you started.

Familiarise yourself with local law:

When we talk about local law, we're referring to any laws that apply to your local area. For example, in America, you could be affected by both state and federal law. Knowing what the laws are will help you to ensure that you comply with them.

Familiarise yourself with regulations in your industry:

Each industry has a different set of rules and regulations, and some have more than others. Most of the time, you won't need to worry too much, as long as you're complying with data protection laws, but in some heavily regulated industries, such as finance and healthcare, there may be additional rules that you'll need to comply with. Be aware of what these are, and do your best to avoid falling foul of them.

Keep abreast of international law:

Even if you're a small business, it's important to keep an eye on the latest developments in international law because it's not uncommon for one precedent to spark changes in other regions. Just because something doesn't affect you yet, it doesn't mean that you're safe forever.

Consider creating internal social media protocols:

Fighting regulation with regulation might seem counterintuitive, but it can help you to ensure that you're in full compliance. For example, if you're required to report any side effects within twenty-four hours, consider an internal protocol that requires you to report them sooner. That way, even if you fail to comply with your internal protocol, you'll still be within the law.

If in doubt, ask a lawyer:

If you're a larger business, then you may want to consider working with a specialist. Whilst this can be seen as an expense, it's often necessary, and it's a great way to ensure peace of mind. You might never see a return, but that's a good thing. If you're not fined by the FTC then it was worth it. Some lawyers also offer free or discounted rates, particularly to start-ups.

Don't worry too much:

It might sound like it's all doom and gloom, but try not to worry. It's pretty rare for a company to be hit by a fine for non-compliance. As long as you have the best interests of your customers at heart, you're unlikely to run up against a problem. It's also primarily large, international companies that get levied with fines, probably because it sets an example to the thousands of other companies who are making similar mistakes. If you work for a small or medium sized business, you'll probably be alright.

CHAPTER FIFTEEN: IMAGE

FOR ANY BUSINESS, image is everything. Some companies spend millions on marketing and advertising, and the branding industry is all about public image.

Social networking provides brands with a way to establish their public image, but it can also tarnish reputations beyond repair. I see social networking sites as the great leveller. Companies are no longer able to lie about their products because the masses will find out and rebel against them.

Instead, they must use social networking sites to enhance their honesty and to speak with an authentic voice about the things that they're passionate about. People do business with people they like, and they buy from brands whose values they align with. Before the rise of social networking, companies told their stories through radio ads and TV spots, and it was difficult for customers to complain. Now, with the rise of social networking, there are more ways than ever for brands to communicate with consumers, but there are also more ways for consumers to vent their frustration.

Let's look at a case study.

Case Study: *McDonald's Has a #McFail*
Classification: *Image*

What Happened:

In early 2012, McDonald's was forced to pull its #McDStories campaign from Twitter after a backlash from users. The hashtag, which was promoted using paid advertisements, was supposed to encourage consumers to share positive stories about the fast food giant.

However, it didn't go according to plan. Disgruntled Twitter users hijacked the hashtag to post their own stories. Because it's impossible to filter negativity from a hashtag, the company was eventually forced to cancel the campaign.

Most tweets were posted by health and animal rights activists with one tweet reading: "My father used to bring us to McDonald's as a reward when we were kids. Now he's horribly obese and has diabetes. Lesson learned. #McDStories"

How it Could've Been Avoided:

You could argue that the campaign was poorly planned and that McDonald's should've expected a backlash. After all, it's hardly the first time that consumers have rebelled against a fast food conglomerate. Still, McDonald's reacted quickly, presumably because they had a plan in place, and they pulled the campaign before it caused any lasting damage.

So it's clear that social networking can affect the way that you're perceived. In fact, 62.3% of survey respondents agree that social networking influences their perception of brands. I can tell you anecdotally that I've bought from (and boycotted) brands after following them on social media. On top of that, a surprisingly high percentage (18.6%) of survey respondents have noticed brands acting strangely, which raises an interesting question: how exactly do you measure how people perceive you?

One option is sentiment analysis, which relies on processing large amounts of publicly viewable data – such as all tweets containing the name of the brand – and using an algorithm to determine whether the posts are positive, negative or neutral. By tracking this over time, brands can see whether their marketing campaigns are affecting their public image.

Now, I'm not a fan of sentiment analysis. To do it correctly, you need huge amounts of data, which not every brand has access to, and automation doesn't always work. You could do it manually, but that takes a lot of time and you'd lose the ability to monitor sentiment in real time. As with most forms of analysis, you should take it with a pinch of salt.

Besides, if everything goes wrong and you're coming under fire, you don't need a sophisticated sentiment analysis tool to tell you that your brand has been damaged. Let's take a look at another case study. This one shows that small businesses are still at risk, even if the headlines are usually dedicated to multinationals.

Case Study: *Amy's Social Nightmares*
Classification: *Image*

What Happened:

After being featured on an episode of Gordon Ramsay's Kitchen Nightmares in which Ramsay walked out and the owners chased disgruntled diners outside shouting "Fuck you, you piece of shit!" and "You little pansy, get out of here.", Amy's Baking Company Bakery Boutique & Bistro went into a meltdown[53].

The company's two founders, Samy and Amy Bouzaglo, started posting from their Facebook page to defend themselves against the negativity that was heading their way from Yelp, Reddit, Facebook and Twitter. Unfortunately, they didn't handle it very well.

Here are just a few of their replies:

I AM NOT STUPID. ALL OF YOU ARE YOU JUST DO NOT KNOW GOOD FOOD. IT IS NOT UNCOMMON TO RESELL THINGS. WALMART DOES NOT MAKE THEIR ELECTRONICS OR TOYS, SO LAY OFF!!!!!

TO REDDIT. I FORBID YOU FROM SPREADING YOUR HATE ON THAT SITE. THIS IS MY FACEBOOK, AND I AM NOT ALLOWING

[53] See: http://www.buzzfeed.com/ryanhatesthis/this-is-the-most-epic-brand-meltdown-on-facebook-ever#.sx3Rkgp3B

YOU TO USE MY COMPANY ON YOUR HATE FILLED PAGE.

You people are all shit. Yelp shit, Reddits shit. Every shit. Come to here, I will fucking show you all.

How it Could've Been Avoided:

To me, this just seems like common sense. I don't understand how anybody could think that posting crazy messages would help to diffuse the situation. A better approach would have been to offer considered, polite responses to each of the messages that they received and to have maintained as much radio silence as possible until the initial outcry about the TV programme was over. Of course, you should also try to avoid running your business in such a way that it causes a public outcry in the first place.

There's another thing to think about if you're trying to maintain a positive public image, and that's the quality of your content. If you're putting out low-quality content, people will notice. In fact, 28.9% of our survey respondents have spotted poor quality content in action.

In some cases, you can get away with this. For example, if you're trying to maintain a presence on YouTube then it's better to create multiple low-budget videos than it is to create just one in a higher quality. This is particularly relevant to small businesses because nobody expects them to have a huge budget to cover production costs.

Interestingly, 1 in 5 (21.8%) of our respondents believe that other people judge them based upon the brands that they interact with. If you follow a racist organisation, for example, then other people are likely to make snap decisions about your character.

Option	Responses
The way brands look and feel on social media affects my perception of them	62.26%
I've noticed a brand acting strangely/out of character on social media	18.58%
The brands I choose to interact with on social affect people's opinions of me	21.77%
I've noticed a brand using low quality images, video or copy	28.88%

(Source: Survey)

Ultimately, using social networking sites is all about curating a public image. Many of the mistakes that people make could be avoided if they treated themselves like brands and worried about their public image.

Whether you like it or not, we're all obsessed with our image. That's why people wear make-up and why they dress up in their best clothes for a night out. We're exactly the same when it comes to social networking. We try to accentuate the best and downplay the worst, and it can sometimes take its toll as we start to believe each other's lies and to feel as though our own lives pale in comparison.

Let's take a look at one last case study, and then we'll round off this chapter with a few tips on safeguarding your public image whilst using social networking sites.

Case Study: *NYPD Has A #myNYPD Fail*
Classification: *Image*

What Happened:

This case study is surprisingly similar to the McDonald's #McFail debacle, which we talked about earlier in this chapter. Here, the New York Police Department asked people to tweet their #myNYPD photos, expecting people to join in by sharing stories about how the police department has helped them. No such luck.

Whilst the hashtag was used by a number of genuine well-wishers, people also used it to post allegations of corruption and to share photographs of police brutality. The New York Police Department later went on record to say, "You take the good with the bad."[54]

How it Could've Been Avoided:

Again, an organisation such as NYPD, which is usually quite savvy when it comes to technology, ought to have been prepared for a backlash. That said, they dealt with it in a professional manner and with a no-nonsense approach, like you'd expect from the police. They were also lucky enough to have a passionate army of followers who leapt to their defence, demonstrating one of the unique advantages of a branded community.

---

[54] See: http://www.prweek.com/article/1291343/latest-social-media-fail-case-study-mynypd

Let's take a look at how you can protect your public image in the era of social networking.

Monitor in real-time:

Real-time monitoring is the process of using a dashboard tool, such as TweetDeck or Hootsuite, to view specific updates in real time, as and when they're posted. By setting up real-time monitoring for your hashtag, your brand name or your campaign name, you'll be able to detect any negativity as soon as it appears. At the very least, this can act as an early warning system – a useful thing to have in the fast-paced world of digital marketing.

Build a community:

The NYPD case study showed how a community can be a powerful ally when you're under attack. It takes time and dedication to build a community, but once you have one, it'll stick around.

Test campaigns before deploying them:

Be sure to test your campaigns before you fully commit to them. If you dip your toe into the water, you might find sharks. Better to lose a toe than a leg! This is particularly important if you're running a campaign like McDonald's and the NYPD.

Be prepared for anything:

Seriously, be prepared for anything. People are unpredictable, and social networking is an extension of their unpredictable personalities. They also like to get offended. A great example was when Femfresh came under fire for using the word "froo-froo," instead of "vagina[55]." By trying not to offend people, they managed to offend people.

Always have a plan:

Have a response plan drawn up and ready to go, just in case. That way, if everything goes wrong then you'll know exactly what to do. You could even consider practice runs and drills, just to be sure that everyone understands their responsibilities.

---

[55] See: http://www.huffingtonpost.co.uk/2012/06/21/women-femfresh-vagina-outrage_n_1616156.html

CHAPTER SIXTEEN: NEGATIVITY

NEGATIVITY IS INTERESTING because sometimes brands deserve it. If your product isn't up to scratch or if there are failings in the service that you're offering, then your customers have a right to complain. Instead of treating this as a problem, you should embrace it. You can learn from them, and you can try to solve the problem and to turn them back into happy customers.

Over half (59.8%) of survey respondents expected brands to respond to complaints on social networking sites, but not all of them took it to the next level. Just over a quarter of them (26.59%) have actually posted a complaint, although that's still a relatively high percentage of people.

As for me, I complain all the time, but it's mostly a low-level badgering of brands because of their terrible spelling and grammar. I even convinced Old El Paso to remove an unnecessary apostrophe from their packaging.

Option	Responses
I've complained about a brand on social media	26.59%
I expect brands to respond to complaints on social media	59.80%
I've heard stories about brands reacting badly to negativity	39.08%
If a brand addressed my complaint, I'd consider buying from them again	48.31%

(Source: Survey)

Unfortunately for brands, if you give people a reason to be negative, they'll be negative. If your product is poor, if you source your stock unethically or if you're perceived negatively already then you're in for a lot of trouble.

Thing is, your reputation will suffer either way. At least if you join the conversation, you can try to offer a solution. Negativity is a way of life. If there's no negativity, then there's probably no positivity either. Don't dismiss it. Learn from it, and use this new type of honest customer feedback, which was never available previously, to improve your business.

Case Study: *Turning Things Around for Colour B4*
Classification: *Negativity*

What Happened:

Colour B4 is a hair colour remover and a former client of mine. I used to help out with their social media presence, but it quickly became apparent that there was a wider problem. People didn't trust the company's promises, and there were plenty of detractors who posted complaints about the product.

We decided to counter it by showcasing the real experiences of our users We amassed over 400,000 views on YouTube by approaching people and offering to host their videos in exchange for a free sample. We also offered free samples in exchange for before and after photos, and hundreds of people responded.

Eventually, we managed to build a community of people who swore by the product and who used it all of the time. They started sharing tips that we'd never thought of, and people would come to our defence if they saw a complaint.

How it Could've Been Improved:

Colour B4 shot themselves in the foot with their TV ad, which portrayed the product as miraculous. It wasn't miraculous. It was just pretty good, when used correctly. This approach was great for short-term sales, but it also led to lots of disappointment.

Instead, they should've started with user-generated content to tell the real stories of the people who used the product. I've always thought it's better to exceed expectations than to fail to meet them.

This Colour B4 case study shows that even if you are facing negativity, it's not impossible to change public perception. The key to social media marketing is to be authentic; telling the true stories of the people who use your product is a great way for you to show that authenticity.

There are plenty of reasons why you might come under fire, and we've touched upon some of them already. Common reasons for negativity include environmental or human rights concerns, disagreements with prominent figures at the company, or a problem with the product or service.

The key to dealing with negativity is to turn it into positivity. The very best brands actively seek out detractors – for example, by looking for tweets that use the brand's name but that don't mention their Twitter handle – and try to placate them before they go any further.

Case Study: *O2 Responds to a Network Outage*
Classification: *Negativity*

What Happened:

O2, a British telecommunications company (and a former client of mine), took to Twitter to offer customer service to people who were affected by a network outage. They responded with humour when it was appropriate. Whilst they did deal with negativity professionally, their responses also helped to entertain their other followers.

They were able to do this, in part, because they'd already spent time and resources building relationships with their followers, and so people were happy to come to their defence. When one follower asked, "Why is O2 responding to offensive tweets?", the company replied, "They're not so bad. Sometimes all they need is a little care and attention :)".

How it Could Be Repeated:

Situations like a network outage are impossible to truly avoid, and they usually can't even be predicted. Instead, you need to prepare a plan that you can follow if something does happen, so that you're able to move nimbly in times of crisis. You can bet that O2 had a plan in place for network outages. After all, it's the worst thing that can happen if you're a telecommunications company. You'd need to need to plan everything from the rapid response of engineers to the deployment of communications.

We've already talked about people's expectations when it comes to complaining on social, but as we saw in chapter fifteen with Amy's Baking Company Bakery Boutique & Bistro, not all companies are able to use social networking to diffuse a situation. In fact, 39.1% of survey respondents have heard stories of brands reacting badly, and so has everyone who's reading this book.

Despite that, it's not all doom and gloom, as 48.31% of respondents said that if a brand addressed their complaint then they'd consider buying from them again. I've done this, but out of necessity and not out of choice. Take public transportation company Arriva, for example. Their services are terrible, at least where I live, and I've even written a poem about it called *Arriva #800/850*, which you can check out in *Eyes Like Lighthouses When the Boats Come Home*, my book of poetry.

I've complained to Arriva in a number of different ways, including in a blog post and in a letter of complaint. I've also complained about them on social networking sites. They gave me a free weekly pass once, and it's true that I still use their services. I have to, otherwise I can't get to work.

Ultimately, negativity towards brands is one of the predominant themes in *Social Paranoia*, and it's a subject that we've discussed at length throughout the book. It's easy to see how dealing with negativity, even when you're convinced that your product is perfect, could lead to feelings of paranoia.

And unfortunately, unlike hacks, leaks, and some of the other topics that we've talked about, you're never going to be able to fully protect yourself against negativity. It's a part of life. To ignore it or to avoid dealing with it is the act of a company with a fear of facing reality.

Let's close this chapter with one final case study and a few quick tips to help you to deal with any negativity that comes your way.

Case Study: *Buffer Responds to a Hack*
Classification: *Negativity*

What Happened:

When software application Buffer was hacked in 2013, they could have panicked. But they didn't. They took to social networking sites to post an announcement, saying: "Hey everyone! We greatly apologise for this big mess we've created. Buffer has been hacked."

The statement also included advice on how to protect yourself, and it was signed off by a guy called Leo. Including the name of an employee was a great way to remind people that in the end, we're only human, and the informative post helped to diffuse any remaining negativity.

How it Could Be Repeated:

You can find out more about hacks and leaks in chapter three. When it comes to Buffer's response, they did a fantastic job of communicating with their users, and they left little to be desired. This is a great example of how an appropriate reaction helped a company to avoid disaster.

Here are a few top tips for dealing with negativity:

Make sure that your product isn't at fault:

Too often, the problem lies with your product or service. Make sure that whatever you're selling is at its best, so that you're not giving people a reason to complain. It's hard enough to deal with negativity without having a crappy product or service to worry about, too.

Have a response protocol:

Prepare for negativity in advance, and decide how you're going to deal with it. Your response protocol should include your official position on common complaints, your stance on offering refunds and replacements, and the escalation process if the issue can't be resolved.

Try to help people:

This should be your ultimate goal. You're not trying to sell to people who've posted a complaint; you're trying to help them. Keep this in mind, and do everything in your power to resolve the issue.

Act upon feedback:

If people report problems, make sure that you investigate so you can try to stop them from happening again. There's no point just blindly offering free replacements if the same problem keeps occurring. Instead, try to fix the problem so that you're not spending as much money sending out replacements!

Don't take it too personally:

It's common for people to think highly of their company, so it can be unpleasant to deal with complaints. Remember not to take the criticism personally, and that at the end of the day, it's just a job. Don't burn yourself out!

CLOSURE

DON'T BE AFRAID. We're almost at the end. By now, you've learned all about social paranoia, and we've talked about why you're right to be paranoid. In primitive man, paranoia could save a life, and so we've evolved to be paranoid by our very nature.

And this is a good thing. After all, if you're paranoid about security then you're more likely to use strong passwords. This, in turn, makes it less likely that you'll suffer a hack, and so your paranoia is helping you to stay safe. Of course, then when nothing happens, people can accuse you of being paranoid. That's something you're going to have to live with.

By now, you should know all of the tips and tricks that you need to protect yourself on social networking sites. If you start to implement them then you can reduce the odds of an incident. But you can never remove that possibility entirely, so be sure to have a plan in place to cope with a situation if it arises.

In the end, social networking is a lot of fun and it's a great way to stay in touch with people, but it's a bit like learning to drive. You need to know the rules and regulations if you want to be a safe social networker.

When you write a book called *Social Paranoia*, you start to become paranoid yourself. In many ways, I'm setting myself up as a target. If you're a hacker, I can see why it might be fun to try to hack someone who wrote about avoiding being hacked. Please don't do that.

Likewise, please don't cyberstalk me looking for mistakes because we all make them. It's how we deal with our mistakes that makes us who we are.

Stay safe out there.

Dane Cobain
24th July 2016

APPENDIX: SURVEY METHODOLOGY

WHILST A NUMBER of external sources were used during the creation of *Social Paranoia*, the basic statistics were the results of a survey that was carried out during the summer of 2015.

Option	Responses
17 or younger	0.66%
18-20	4.34%
21-29	28.46%
30-39	32.14%
40-49	17.34%
50-59	11.97%
60 or older	5.09%

(Source: Survey)

The survey was seeded through social networking profiles and via word of mouth, and it was heavily promoted through my book blog, SocialBookshelves.com. It ran for approximately six months.

Across the six-month period, 1,066 survey responses were recorded with 911 people completing every question in the survey. The majority of respondents were aged twenty-one to twenty-nine (29.5%) or thirty to thirty-nine (32.1%), with just 0.7% of respondents aged seventeen or younger.

Option	Responses
Female	70.90%
Male	29.00%
Other	0.10%

(Source: Survey)

Interestingly, there was a gender disparity amongst our respondents with 70.9% identifying as female and 29% as male. Fortunately, an analysis of the data found no significant differences between men and women when it came to the answers that they posted, suggesting that social paranoia can potentially affect us all, regardless of race, ethnicity or religious background.

This is further supported when it comes to the geographic breakdown of survey respondents. Despite the fact that 93.4% of respondents were based in the UK, this doesn't seem to have influenced the data to any significant degree.

Option	Responses
UK	93.39%
United States	4.63%
Europe	0.85%
South America	0.00%
Asia Pacific	0.09%
Africa	0.28%
Other	0.76%

(Source: Survey)

Likewise, there were no major differences when it came to the employment status of the respondents. Approximately two thirds of respondents were in either part-time or full-time employment, with the remainder of people either unemployed (21.3%), disabled (6.3%) or retired

(4.9%).

Option	Responses
Employed, working full-time	40.98%
Employed, working part-time	26.53%
Not employed, looking for work	6.89%
Not employed, not looking for work	14.35%
Retired	4.91%
Disabled, not able to work	6.33%

(Source: Survey)

Our survey respondents also reported a wide range of education levels, which may be due to their differing ages. The results showed that 5.6% of respondents dropped out of high school, whilst 22.9% reported a high school degree, such as an A-level, as their highest certificate of education.

Option	Responses
Less than high school degree	5.57%
High school degree or equivalent	22.85%
Some college but no degree	29.93%
Associate degree	4.72%
Bachelor degree	26.06%
Graduate degree	10.86%

(Source: Survey)

Meanwhile, approximately 30% of respondents studied at college but didn't complete a degree, a further 26% of people received a bachelor degree, and the final 10.9% of people went on to study a graduate degree.

The final question focused on a factor that might influence social paranoia. We asked whether people identified as an introvert or an extrovert. The number of introverts was surprisingly high at 51.5%; meanwhile, 20.7% of people considered themselves to be extroverts, and the remaining 27.8% of people said they were neither.

Option	Responses
Introvert	51.46%
Extrovert	20.74%
Neither	27.80%

(Source: Survey)

ACKNOWLEDGEMENTS

A BOOK LIKE THIS doesn't write itself. I couldn't have done it without the army of survey respondents and the long list of friends and family members who knew what I was up to and who kept their eyes peeled for potential case studies. You guys are great.

Then there's the inimitable Pam Elise Harris, my faithful editor who picks apart my manuscripts and then helps me put them back together again, for which I'm immensely grateful. Any mistakes that you see are mine, and mine alone; all of the mistakes that you don't see are thanks to Pam.

Thanks also to you, the reader, and to all of the supporters who've read and shared my work throughout the years. There are too many to name, but that includes Donna Woodings, Nick Reffin, Neil Denham, Olga and Alan Woodings and Heather and Dave Clarke. You guys are awesome.

Stay social!

JOIN THE CONVERSATION

Social networking can be a lot of fun, despite the risks. If you're feeling brave enough, join me on your social network of choice or tweet @DaneCobain.

danecobain.com
twitter.com/danecobain
facebook.com/danecobainmusic

Authors need reviews like animals need food. Please feed your favourite authors by posting reviews on Amazon and Goodreads. Seriously, it helps!

MORE GREAT READS
FROM DANE COBAIN

No Rest for the Wicked (Supernatural Thriller) When the Angels attack, there's *No Rest for the Wicked*. Cobain's debut novella, a supernatural thriller, follows the story of the elderly Father Montgomery as he tries to save the world—or at least, his parishioners—from mysterious, spectral assailants.

Eyes Like Lighthouses When the Boats Come Home (Poetry) *Eyes Like Lighthouses* is Dane Cobain's first book of poetry, distilled from the sweat of a thousand memorised performances in this reality and others. It's not for the faint-hearted.

Former.ly (Literary Fiction) When Dan Roberts starts his new job at Former.ly, he has no idea what he's getting into. The site deals in death. Its users share their innermost thoughts, which are stored privately until they die. Then, their posts are shared with the world, often with unexpected consequences.

Discover more books
at <u>danecobain.com</u>.

www.ingramcontent.com/pod-product-compliance
Lightning Source LLC
Chambersburg PA
CBHW031242050326
40690CB00007B/921